— The Modern Art of —

BRUJERÍA

A Beginner's Guide to Spellcraft,
Medicine Making, and Other Traditions
of the Global South

Lou Florez

Published by:
ULYSSES PRESS
PO Box 3440
Berkeley, CA 94703
www.ulyssespress.com

ISBN: 978-1-64604-319-4
Library of Congress Control Number: 2021946379

Printed in the United States by Versa Press
10 9 8 7 6 5 4 3 2

Acquisitions editor: Ashten Evans
Managing editor: Claire Chun
Editor: Anne Healey
Proofreader: Barbara Schultz
Front cover design and illustration: Adriana C. García Soto/fiverr
Interior design: what!design @ whatweb.com
Production: Jake Flaherty, Yesenia Garcia Lopez

CONTENTS

INTRODUCTION

As we elevate, we lift.

"Mijo, I'm wearing some of that holy water you have—you know, the one I found in your car."

"Mom, I don't have any holy water in my car, what are you talking about?"

"Mijo, you know, the one that's hanging on the window."

Grabbing me by the hand, she charged through congregations of hungry chickens and hip-high grasses toward the faded powder-blue Buick '88, or "the boat," as I called it. Flinging the passenger door open and pointing to the window, she said, "¿Que es eso?" (What is that?)

My twenties, like my car, were filled with a mélange of crystals, tingsha bells, charred chicken's feet tied to the rearview mirror for protection, and an assortment of other miscellaneous "bruje" crap scattered across the seats and cup holders. What I thought I needed then and what my practice looks like now are dramatically different. An Elder once said that the Craft matures us and we mature the Craft.

"¿Que es eso?" Prodding with her right index finger, she drew my attention to the glass vase suction-cupped to the window. I had already had a "coming out of the broom closet" conversation with her earlier in the summer, so anything and everything had the potential to be "brujería" in her eyes. Now, sticking her finger to the bottom of the glass and anointing her wrists with water, she rubbed vigorously and smelled.

What she had thought was holy water was in reality the remnants from the flowers I had recently discarded. I began to explain, but to her it didn't matter. Holiness was part of its essential nature regardless of whether it had been "blessed." We laughed and anointed each other with sweet benedictions till it ran dry.

What makes a water holy?

My mother was a Bruja.

She wasn't the classical black-hat-wearing, skin the color of snot, soul-stealing version as seen in the *Wizard of Oz*, nor the modern, cool, fantastically gifted, chic version like the sisters on *Charmed*—she was a woman who acknowledged everyone in the room, and to acknowledge is to have a stake in a person's life (at least in that moment). She created connections between and among people, narratives, foods, and tchotchkes. She animated life; that is to say, brought life to life— brought things to a state of becoming-ness. That was my mother, the Bruja.

A Bruja(e)[1] is a woman, a person, a being, a consciousness that in-animates (pours soul into) the world. They are a becoming-ness— standing at the edge of arrival, a quickening change that starts internally and ripples out manifesting in a Universe that is surreal—a juicier, sweeter, more succulent rendition of a moment than the one that it precedes.

---

1 A prominent aspect of gender conversations within Spanish-speaking populations has been the recent use of the letter *-x* by Latinx communities in the United States as a gender-neutral ending for nouns and pronouns. The letter *-e* has historically been used for this purpose by Caribbeans and South and Central Americans, but because of positional privileging of living in the states, there is a movement to codify *-x* as the legitimate gender-neutral ending within Spanish. Since my politics, allyship, and support are in alignment with Spanish from the Global South, I use *-e* in my writings.

My mother passed on December 6, 2020, at the age of eighty-five.

There are parts of me that are just awakening to this loss like the phantom pains of limbs that are invisible. Through text messages, emails, phone calls, and letters, her families of heart and communities of soul have reached out to share memories—places where their lives were changed through their interactions.

A Bruja(e) is a woman, a person, a being, a consciousness that is re-membered. That is to say, a being comprised of the memories of all those who have met them, scattered across their souls. Long after their physical passing, these aspects live in the cells of those they have encountered. They become the internalized voice that speaks of experiences not our own, the wisdoms of lives lived in totality. What is the opposite of a carcinogen? A Bruja(e) is like that.

In the spring of 2015, I was on Instagram and happened upon a post graphically displaying the charred remains of two indigenous women. The caption described how in Peru, the Office of the Inquisition was internalized as a governmental agency charged with hunting Brujas— that is to say, those who are threatening societal norms, values, or hierarchies. The legacies of the Inquisition in the discourses of magic, witchcraft, and Brujería are inexorably linked to histories of conquest and genocide.

A Bruja(e) is a woman, a person, a being, a consciousness that lives on the periphery, the outskirts, the borderlands, but makes their life the center. They are the dreamers, artists, activists, thinkers, and medicine makers who are journeying to create something new because there are no incentives for them in the present. Those who live on the outskirts are the builders of new cities.

What Is Brujería, Really?

Brujería(s) are a multitude of practices, traditions, and spiritual workings stemming from across the Caribbean and the Americas based not on religious ideologies or beliefs in gods/goddesses or other intermediaries but on a personal connection to one's own power and the engagement of the physical environment and natural world. Magic, within these contexts, is not exterior to the self or based on the recitation of "power" words or formulas but is the activation of the inner soul force vibrating in harmony, consenting to our workings, with the vibrations of the world to produce lasting, poignant change. Brujería, at its core, is rooted in an understanding of our environments, both urban and rural and everywhere in between, and how to build and be in relationship to land and location.

The peoples who created what we now think of as "brujería" did not, themselves, identify under that label. Before conquest, more than one thousand tribes populated North and South America. Following the landing of Columbus in 1492, the Spanish, Portuguese, English, and French colonized North, Central, and South America and the Caribbean, and they created large-scale plantations, which they populated by kidnapping and enslaving Africans. An estimated 22 million people were taken to the Americas and the Caribbean between 1502 and 1866. Even after their emancipations, these communities have received very little support or acknowledgment for their role in the histories of the Americas and often self-describe as having been "disappeared" or made "invisible." The Spanish alone from 1492 to 1824 transplanted 1.86 million Spanish settlers to their colonies in the Americas. These statistics and dates, while numerous, don't account for the Jewish, North African, Middle Eastern, and Asian peoples who have immigrated to these areas throughout the centuries. All of these voices, cultures, and ways of working with Spirit have been labeled demonic, unchristian, uncivilized, and thus "brujería" or witchcraft.

Even if there ever were such a thing, there is no pure or perfect tradition or spellcraft. There is no one way of practicing and creating spells, ceremonies, or rituals. It is my hope to share not just the recipes but why and how people formulate—the Spirit, the anima or life-imbuing forces that animate the work, as well as the techniques for moving energy, life-force, and Spirit.

One of the major differences between Brujería and other global witchcraft traditions is not just the diversity of cultures and their wisdoms of histories, botanical essences, cycles and rhythms of nature, and engagement of their spiritual landscapes, but also the bioregional diversities of plant, animal, and mineralogical beings across the New World. As migration, displacement, and interactions occurred, peoples' traditions and medicines transformed to accommodate not just the new environments but the Spirits that were and are alive within them.

Tenets

With this context in mind, I would like to offer some tenets that unite these various heritages and traditions.

★ Spirit and spirits exist.[2]
★ Everything in existence has a Spirit.
★ Our Spirits can affect physical reality.

---

2 The word *Spirit* refers to the emanating life-force or anima found within every aspect of creation, while *spirits* refers to individual entities or beings.

★ "Magic" is a practice of tangible prayer that builds relationships with and between plant, mineral, and animal beings and harmonizes them with our desire or will.

★ "Magic" is not a cure-all or a substitute for being fully engaged in our lives.

★ The remedy for any spiritual, mental, or emotional imbalance can be found within us and our physical environments.

★ Brujas only need themselves and their Spirits. Everything else is just a support.

Chapter 1

AWAKENING THE BRUJA WITHIN

Grounding, Centering, Sensing, Gathering

The focus of our work in this chapter will be exploring methods and techniques for understanding what energy is and how to sense it in ourselves and our bodies; gathering and harnessing it within ourselves and our environment; and finally, how to move our attention-focus-consciousness-energy both internally and in the world. This is the foundational base that all other Brujería arts are built upon.

Setting Up Your Brujería Lab Journal

Start a fresh journal and label it "Brujería Lab." This will be the place where you can experiment, record your findings, and create community both with me and with the cohort of those who are reading the text simultaneously with you. It can be a living archive—an animated spell for those generations to come.

On this first page, write the heading "Brujería Exercise: Recognizing the Bruja(e)s." Journal about the following questions. Please explore the definition of journaling by creating something meaningful for you—this is yours, your Brujería. Allow yourself to experiment with how you define "writing" and "texts" by drawing, collaging, referencing art, music, scent, texture—any form or medium you are called to voice the experience.

Question 1: What was your first experience of Brujería[3] and brujería?

Question 2: What were your reactions?

Question 3: What is a Bruja(e)?

Question 4: What does a Bruja(e) do?

Question 5: How do Bruja(e)s get treated by their families?

Question 6: How do Bruja(e)s get treated in society?

Question 7: Why would you want to be a Bruja(e)?

WHERE DID WE COME FROM?

Who are the Bruja(e)s you come from, of Blood, Friendship, Inspiration, and Spirit?

Ceremony, ritual, and spellwork are perch-building, a meeting ground where Spirit can enter, land, and then take flight. A bird, like a spell, like Spirit, must consent to settle despite our callings. As medicine makers,

---

3 I use *Brujería* to speak toward real-world changes in our lives based upon our spiritual practices and disciplines versus *brujería*, the sleight-of-hand or smoke-and-mirror theatrics of "Instagram witches" who make it seem like all you have to do is light a candle to have a magnificent life.

THE MODERN ART OF BRUJERÍA

as Bruja(e)s, our work is to create the structures, these in-between spaces for meetings to occur—that is the crossroads where we begin.

As a way of acknowledging and building the perch for our work in this book, inviting you and Spirit within this text, within this spell, within this change, I offer this exercise of libation. Water symbolizes connection, coolness, clarity, and the thresholding energies bridging this world to the next. It is the element of the cosmic womb. It is the one element needed for life and that connects all life on this planet.

Libation, an Offering of Water

Ingredients: a small vessel of water.

Start by taking your right middle finger and sprinkling a little water on the ground during the first seven lines of the libation. This signifies an offering of water to each of these entities and Divinities in your life. After this initial sprinkling, you can put aside the water vessel and sit or stand in a comfortable, meditative position. During the entirety of the process and throughout the remainder of the book, it is important to physically speak your prayers, intentions, and spells in order to activate the potency and power of the mouth to name and create the changes you are seeking.

Cool Water, Fresh Water,

Water for our Indwelling Spirits,

Water to the Divinities of the Crossroads—those Beings who deliver our prayers to the other realms and carry back their replies

Water to the Earth beneath us and to all the Stewards of the Land

Water to the Transcendent Ancestors, those Beings who can remake the Cosmos in the blink of an eye

Water to all the Divinities and Forces of Nature who continually work to uplift humanity

Water again to the Crossroads Divinities to ensure that our manifested prayers and workings arrive with grace, beauty, and sweetness.

We call upon these Forces, the Divinities of elevation and upliftment, to hear our voices and our prayers.

Close the roads and bar the doors to all Negating Forces and Beings.

Avert the Spirits of Poverty, Contention, Conflict, Illness, Disease, Strife, Trauma, Chaos, Litigation, Curses, Envy, Jealousy, Ableism, Racism, Gender and Sexual Discrimination, and Systems of Oppression and all Entities who seek to harm.

We call to you Divinities to make us invisible before these Forces, and wherever they may search, they cannot see me

To the Lineages of our Mothers, to the Lineages of our Fathers, to all the Lineages of Heart, Inspiration, and Spirit, let us never see Death before our time.

We give praise and honor to the Creator, the Great Womb of Light, in which we all arise and are reborn back into.

We give honor and praise to the Transcendent Ancestors who sit at the feet of the Creator and pray continually on our behalf

We give honor and praise to our Spirit Guides, Elevated Masters, Holy Guardians and Protectors, and Evolved Spirit Communities in the Other Realms

We give honor and praise to our Indwelling Spirits, our most Liberated Fully Realized Self who gives us guidance, wisdom, and support as we make our pilgrimages toward our actualization

We give honor and praise to our communities of practice and the medicines that they have taught us.

We ask license and permission this day from all the Medicine Holders, Spirit Workers, Priestesses, Priests, and Officiates who have shown us how to walk in character and good medicine, and we ask that they guide our hands and Spirits as we work.

So it is said, so it is, so it is manifest.

Brujería is more than the Spanish translation of "witch" and "witchcraft." These traditions, both old and new, are practices for transforming surviving into thriving despite intentionally created systems of oppression. They are World Wisdom Practices that are being upheld not in opposition to modernity but as a different path for walking into the future. Why does the West uplift Christianity, Islam, Buddhism, and Hinduism as the only paths toward self-realization, and what does that mean for our experiences and traditions? Who benefits from this positioning?

ENERGETIC BREATHING

Our breath holds our life force, vitality, and consciousness, and as you move throughout the book, there will be places where you literally pour it into your work in order to unify the ingredients and bring them life.

The focus of this meditation is bringing awareness to your thoughts and emotions and learning to work with them as they arise in order to be fully present in the work. This process helps to establish a foundation of peace and tranquility and release all other reactive thoughts and feelings that are not part of the practice.

A simple method for stilling the heart, mind, and Spirit is breathing and softening the inner gaze (being attentive and focused but not mechanical; as a distracting thought or emotion arises, recognize it and return your attention to the breath).

1. Begin by emptying the lungs fully and holding the breath for a count of four.

2. Inhale to a count of four so that the lungs are fully expanded and filled completely (imagine that the breath fills your lungs all the way to the throat and mouth).

3. Hold this breath while counting to four again, keeping the throat open and relaxed.

4. Exhale, counting to four, until you feel the lungs completely empty.

5. Hold the exhale to a count of four, and remember you want the mouth, throat, and chest completely relaxed and not strained.

6. Repeat the process: empty the lungs and hold for a count of four; inhale to a count of four; hold for a count of four; exhale to a count of four; hold for a count of four; inhale to a count of four.

Note: This practice is about finding your personal rhythms, so experiment! Try this practice with both slow and fast counting; the intention is to find a pace that allows you to sit in stillness and comfort. Once you find a pace that is appropriate, count the breath for two to three minutes until you feel quiet and relaxed, and then go back to your normal breathing pattern. At this point you can move on with your spellwork, ritual, or ceremony.

VISUALIZATION (OPENING THE MIND'S EYE) EXPERIMENT

One of the greatest tools that a Bruja(e) has in their arsenal is their ability to visualize—to form and hold mental images. For anyone interested in Brujería, magic, or witchcraft, this discipline is vitally important because it helps you to hold not only the idea but also the energies of what you are working to create. If you can't visualize it, you can't manifest it. Below are a series of exercises that can help develop these skill sets and were part of my magical foundations as I was starting out.

Mariah's Game: This is a fun exercise meant to stimulate the memory and build your ability to recall items on a sensory level.

1. Find someone to randomly pick 15 to 20 small objects and put them on a tray.

2. Concentrate on them for a minute and then cover them with a cloth.

3. Make a list of as many of the items as you can recall.

4. When you cannot remember any more, uncover the tray and compare. Which ones did you remember and which ones did you leave out?

As you start to work with your memory, come back to this exercise to see how much you have grown.

Rubber Ball: Sometimes people have concerns about their ability to hold any shapes or objects in their mind's eye, and this can be an entrance for developing the skill. All muscles atrophy when they aren't used, and our imagination and visualization muscles can do the same.

1. Picture a plain ball with no pattern or color, and try to hold that image in your mind for as long as you can.

2. Once you feel like you have successfully accomplished the task, add color to the image.

3. Finally, add texture to the ball and hold the fully realized image in your visualization.

These first two exercises are great foundations. Next, try playing with it a bit more to see how detailed you can get with your imagination.

Place of Familiarity: In this exercise you will imagine a place that you know with great familiarity and work toward recalling as many sensory details as you can.

1. Pick any place that is easy to recall.

2. Begin by imagining yourself viewing all the details and features of this location as you move throughout the image in your mind. Try to be as specific as you can with colors, textures, shapes, and lighting—you will fully use your senses to explore this memory.

3. If you are able to access the space in your current life, compare your memories to how it appears now. What items did you miss, what things did you notice, and were there any reasons why you noticed them?

MICROCOSMIC ORBIT (COMBINES BREATH AND VISUALIZATION)

This technique originates from Taoist chi-gung practices that help to cultivate and move our internal energies and life force through a combination of breathing techniques and visualization. The term *orbit* here references the circling of energetic light around the body, and this practice is meant to help you gather any stray or wandering energies, unite them with your life force, and raise them from your root energy center to your crown and back again, creating an orbiting energy.

1. Find a comfortable sitting position and start with the breathing meditation on page 11.

2. Bring your attention to the area halfway between your navel and your pubic bones, and visualize your energies there.

3. Exhale completely.

4. As you take a deep breath, begin to visualize a current of golden energy that flows from this midpoint in your body and follow it as it travels beneath the pubic bone to your coccyx (base of the spine).

5. Following this current of energy, it begins to travel up the spine and the back of the neck.

6. As it flows up the neck, now this golden light proceeds up the back of your head and over your crown.

7. From the crown it flows over your forehead and travels to your third eye.

8. At this point you are still inhaling your breath; you will now pause for a count of three before you exhale.

9. Touching your tongue to the soft palate of your mouth (creating a circuit for the energies to travel), slowly let the energy descend over the exterior of your face, over your lips and teeth, and flowing across the top palate.

10. From the top palate the current travels down your tongue and throat, across your lower jaw, over your lower teeth and lip, and down the chin.

11. Continue to follow this channel of light as it radiates down the chin to the throat, down the torso and finally completing the circuit where you began (the area between the navel and the pubic bones).

12. Pause again for another count of three before taking the next inhalation and starting the orbit again.

PROCEDURES FOR ALL RECIPES, SPELLS, AND RITUALS IN THE BOOK

These are the steps and methodologies that you will engage as you work through the remainder of the book.

1. Come to your space in a positive mood and have a clean area to work from because everything you are feeling, thinking about, and putting energies toward will be absorbed by the material.

2. Set up your space both in terms of accessibility (making sure things are easily within reach and sight) as well as curating the music and other sensory experiences, like drink, textures, and even how you curate the ingredients. You want to make the whole environment reverberate with your intention through each of the five senses.

3. Gather all your supplies and check everything twice before you begin because nothing is worse than having to get up several times to find things. As someone who easily forgets where I last stored an item, I can waste 15 minutes looking for scissors. It also takes time to get back into the energetic flow, and that start-stop pattern can suck all the juice and enjoyment out of the process.

4. Begin to center yourself and charge your energies with the breathing exercise (page 11) and the microcosmic orbit (page 15).

5. The next steps seem menial, but they are about honoring, asking consent, and giving purpose to each of the ingredients. Remember, it doesn't have to be a big production; it's about greeting the consciousnesses of everything your engage with.

Start by spiritually cleaning and honoring the jar and all the tools you will be using. Some people like to take some premade Agua Florida or other spiritual waters and wipe down everything to cleanse, smooth, and cut away any negative energy. Next you might say a verbal intention aligning the instrument with the purpose of the working and running it through incense or smudge. As an example, let's start with the jar. As an option for the smudge I might consider burning a mixture of copal, tobacco, and yarrow on an incense charcoal in a fireproof dish.

Chapter 2

BÓVEDAS AND AGUA FLORIDAS

The Arts of Ancestral Veneration, Mediumship, and Working with the Dead

Bóvedas, Creating the Ancestral Altar

Bóveda loosely translates from Spanish as "vault" and carries a double meaning of being a secure space to hold treasures as well as a room or building with arched roofs—holy places with the architecture of a sacred space. Put together, it points to a safe space where you can hold your treasures and let your prayers and your consciousness ascend. As you move forward, remember that you are welcoming Spirit internally to assist you in creating the change you are seeking externally.

CREATING THE BÓVEDA IN YOUR HOME

The physical bóveda or spiritual vault for your ancestral venerations can be created on any surface, from the floor, to a table, to a shelf on a bookcase or fireplace, or in a closet or cabinet. Created to be a physical portal or doorway for the departed to enter our homes and spaces, it acts as a focal point for waking up, evoking, and building relationships with our beloved dead.

Preparation

Find an area that is quiet, peaceful, and not easily reached by pets or infants. As a suggestion, you might find a space in a corner of a room or in areas of low traffic where you can erect your altar to ensure that items aren't unintentionally moved by family or guests. Start by thoroughly cleaning the area both physically as well as spiritually with any of the Agua Florida recipes (Agua Florida is a spiritual perfume that attracts positive forces, cools and calms the indwelling Spirit, and repels negativity and negative forces), and spiritually cleanse the space using incense. An example of an incense blend that could be used for this purpose would be tobacco, Mexican sage, rosemary, copal, and frankincense. Finally, demarcate the area with a line of cascarilla (a white chalk made from powdered eggshells; it can be bought at most botanicas) to ensure that the only entities coming into your home are the ancestors that you intend to call.

KEY ITEMS FOR THE BÓVEDA

Tablecloth: A white or light-colored tablecloth is typically used to circumscribe and calm the spiritual space. Light-colored fabrics reflect heat and negativity and vibrationally uplift the area.

Flowers: A life-giving principle on the altar representing our communications, prayers, and intentions with our ancestors, flowers energize and refresh the altar.

Glass or glasses of water: Water refreshes the dead after their long journey; water represents life, vitality, and communication between realms, and it cools, calms, and disperses heat and negative energies. Water also holds the energies of everything it touches and carries our prayers within it.

Candle: Representing illumination and the ability to perceive, sense, and see, fire connects us with the Creator, stands for upliftment and evolution, and is the transforming principle that allows us to ascend to the next level. (See page 154.)

Photos of transcended family: Family is just that—family, however you define it. The biggest piece of advice is to have photos of family who lived good lives and had themselves together. Often people feel like they have to have everyone on the altar, but for this purpose you are asking that the elevated ancestors are present, versus all dead people who are related to you.

Perfumes: If you know of any perfumes or scents that your ancestors loved, consider spraying the altar down with them when you are doing your prayer work as well as keeping a small bottle on the altar to attract them to you. Perfumes elevate, sweeten, and protect, and provide another level of defense on the table. (See page 109.)

Incense: Sacred smoke is a cross-cultural item that supports and assists depending on the intent and kind used.

BUILDING RELATIONSHIPS WITH THE BÓVEDA

Physically attend to this area weekly by cleaning and replacing the waters, refreshing flowers, cleaning the physical altar of any dust, debris, or detritus, and removing any offerings or organic material before it spoils.

Often people like to do a spiritual service for the ancestors by making foods and drinks that they liked, talking about their days at the altar, playing music, and generally sharing their lives with the beloved dead. Those just beginning with these practices often think that they have to have a special reason to speak with the ancestors or that they can only speak with them at the gravesite or ancestral space, but in actuality we have access to them no matter where we are because they exist primarily in our bodies, hearts, and consciousness.

SAMPLE SERVICES

Below are sample prayers that can be said to open the lines of communication and bring forth elevated ancestral presences. Services can be given at any time and on any day of the week, but I find that doing things first thing in the morning on Sundays helps to guide my week. Often I start with these prayers, make offerings, and play music at my altar and talk to them about whatever is on my heart and mind. At the end of the service I give thanks to all those who have shown up, ask that they continue to walk with me and be in my life, and ring a bell to release the energies and come back to everyday awareness.

Honoring the Creator

Creator, I greet you and the new day. I praise the four directions, the elements, and all the energies that continually create the world anew. These forces bring us the resources, medicines, energies, and support to sustain the Earth and all those who live upon it. They bring us all the things that sustain and nourish our Spirits and strengthen our bodies. When you walk with us, we are victorious, and we give homage to the roads that you have created. When you are our ally, nothing can block the power of Spirit. I praise the life-giving principles in Creation. It brings us the food of the forest, the sweet pleasures in existence. I praise the Creator and the Light and Life in the Earth.

Honoring Our Emanating Spirit

Spark of the Source, emanating Spirit that gives life to all things, we ourselves become Manifestation. With the immortal Being alive within us all, we will never die. When the life-giving Spirit arrives on

Earth, we will never die. The same name we give to Destiny is the same name we give to the ones who have saved us. The Spirit of Manifestation has appeared, our friend has returned for our reunion, and our celebration begins. I come to pray at the sacred tree. I come to pray at the tree that carries my prayers to the Ancestors. The celebration has returned. Be the lips of our prayers, be the eyes of our prayers, hear and touch and taste of our prayers. Emanating Spark, remove any obstacles or blockades from our paths and open the ways for the Transcendent Ancestors to arrive.

Holy Guardian Spirit Prayer

Holy Guardian Spirit, attendant who has seen the suffering of my being and the afflictions in my life, do not reject me at my lowest nor depart from my side in my inconstancy or bad character. Give no place for evil to subdue me with the oppressions directed at this mortal body; but take me by my trembling and outstretched hand, and lead me in the way of liberation. Astounding and Beneficent Holy Being of the Creator, the guardian and protector of my body, mind, and Spirit, be in forgiveness for all the times I self-created troubles in this day and all the days of my life. And if I have acted in bad character in any form this day and in the future, please, Holy Guardian, show compassion. Shelter me in this present night and keep me from every affront of the enemy, lest I anger the Creator by any bad choices; and intercede with the Divinities on my behalf, that Spirit might strengthen and shape me into a clean bone for goodness to inhabit.

The Spiritual Guides

Benevolent and thoughtful Spirits, messengers of the Creator, loving sentinels charged with the mission of helping me grow in wisdom and love, I ask that you give me your support as I face each day's decisions. Help me, oh loving guides, have the fortitude of character to resist harmful thoughts and to resist the temptation to listen to the voices of evil entities induce me to err. Illuminate my thoughts and help me recognize those thoughts and behaviors that are regressive. Remove the veil of ignorance from my eyes so I may recognize the places for growth.

To you, _____ (if you know the name of your main guide, you can use it here, and if not, just ask for your spirit guides in general), who I in particular acknowledge as my guide, and to all the other good Spirits who take an interest in my well-being, I pray that I may be worthy of your consideration. You know my needs; I therefore ask that you help me improve my life as I become closer to the Creator.

Rendition of the Prayer of Saint Francis

"Creator, make me an instrument of your peace. Where there is hatred, let me sow love; Where there is injury, pardon; Where there is doubt, faith; Where there is despair, hope; Where there is sadness, joy. O Divinity of the Most High, grant that I may not so much seek to be consoled as to console, to be understood as to understand, to be loved as to love. For it is in giving that we receive. It is in pardoning that we are pardoned. It is in transforming the self that we are truly liberated."

Assignment: Over the next seven days, refresh your bóveda water each morning and take your glass outside and pray. Connect with the sky and heavens, asking that your spiritual guides move closer in your life.

Flowers and Their Meanings and Associations on the Altar

Notice what flowers you are attracted to and who or what they represent to you. Are there specific flowers that are associated with certain memories? What are those memories about? Do the flowers have scents? What attracts you to them? Keep the answers to these questions in mind each time you replace the flowers on your altar and be intentional about which flowers you choose.

White flowers: Represent the recently departed and their evolutionary journey. They help the dead move past the sensory world and signify purity (everything that is not of us is lifted out), light and internal illumination, and the immortality of our Spirits. They open communication with the Creator and our spiritual guides and are helpers that can calm us when we are energetically overwhelmed.

Red flowers: Help us release problems in our lives, take control of situations, see possibilities for victory, and fight negative energies.

Bright flowers: Represent the energetic personality of the deceased, and help turn mourning into release and joy.

Lilies: Signify fresh life, rebirth, sweetness, and joy. They are reminders of the awe-inspiring grace surrounding our lives and the innocence lying underneath the surface of our traumas.

Irises: Represent the rainbow bridge connecting the living with the ancestral realms and their presence in our lives despite them being unseen.

Sunflowers: Aid in upliftment and protection, manifestation, sweetness, and connectivity—sunflowers reflect the illumination and spark of the Creator in our Spirit. They open the doors for spirit guides and ancestors connected with North African, Middle Eastern, and southern Mediterranean regions.

Azucenas/tuberoses: Protects us from negative or misleading spirits and entities as guardian helpers. They sweeten, entice, and enchant and are also engaged as an aphrodisiac when cooking with chocolate.

Roses: Elevate our Spirits and consciousness and help us create bonds, relationships, and connectivity with those living and those who have passed. They promote the centering of our feelings and experiences and are about feeling like you are "in the middle of a rose garden."

Marigolds: Represent transitions, transformation, solar blessings, rebirth, and the afterlife. They are considered flowers of the dead in Central and South American communities.

Daisies: Represent marriage, fertility, childbirth, love, and first crushes.

Gladiolas: Signify faithfulness, remembrance, role models, and courage.

Carnations: Represent admiration, luck, purification, and gratitude.

Agua Florida

Floral waters like Agua Florida, Lotion Pompeia, Kolonia 1800, Agua de Sandalo, Agua de Violetas, Agua de Rosas, and Kolonia 1800 Tobacco fall under the category of sweetening, cooling, balancing, and elevation work. As we become attuned to how we hold our energies and how easy it is to become overwhelmed, exhausted, hot-headed, hot-tempered, chaotic, and displaced within ourselves in everyday life, we start to look for tools that can counter, rebalance, and reinvigorate ourselves. (As a side note, Agua Florida means "floral water" and is not water from the state of Florida as the name might suggest.)

Scent shapes the way we perceive our world, and perfumery arts have played significant roles not just in our shared history but in every aspect of our lives, especially the spiritual. From roses to rotten meat, Spirit and spirits have often been associated with fragrances as they emanate, and spiritual perfumery engages the energetics of fragrance and how to manifest specific conditions with their uses.

Agua Florida, or Florida Water, like most of the various scents listed above, did not start off as a spiritual perfume but was incorporated into Brujería to invite Spirit internally, into our environment, and to our altars in several ways. First, because the scent is predominantly floral, citrus, and spice, it is considered a spiritually sweet cologne. Sweetening substances are seen as attracting, energizing, and energetically elevating in nature. Sweetness also serves as a protective force because negative and low-vibration entities want to stay in their vibration and do not want to be elevated. You can imagine this working in the same way as when you are in a bad mood and the last person you want to be around is someone super cheerful—that is how Agua Florida works spiritually.

Second, as the scent became popular, more people became associated with it and used it throughout their lives. Scent is one of the fastest ways of bringing up the memory of a person, place, and experience, and if we are really opening a portal within for Spirit to enter, we draw on all the memories and associations we have with the energy we want to emanate.

Brief History of the Scent

Florida Water originated in North America in the mid-nineteenth century, and around this time perfumed alcohols, oils, and other mediums became differentiated from medicinal or allopathic substances, drawing from the inspirations of medicinal/spiritual formulas like the fourteenth-century Hungarian Water, a rosemary-based fragrance used to promote graceful aging; Lavender Water, a fifteenth-century medicine purported to quiet the nervous system and calm the mind; and Eau de Cologne, a sixteenth-century formula that was not only used as a scent but also had instructions for internal use under the name Aqua Mirabilis (miracle water).

Florida Water was said to combine the properties of all these recipes, and in time most pharmacies across the country had their own version made by the store chemists using synthetic compounds. While the spiritual attributes of the scent profile stayed, the plant material and ways of making it medicinally went out of fashion due to manufacturing and the cost and time of production. Throughout the remainder of the nineteenth century to the present, Florida Water has spread globally, with each culture adding its own take on these recipes. Most notable are the derivations from Peru and Hong Kong.

Florida Water is categorized as a cologne, meaning that the scent itself is citrus-forward, mild spice, and fleeting in terms of its tenacity, or the ability for the scent to stay on the skin or in the environment.

Store-Bought Fragrance Aguas and Energetically Charging Them

Store-bought aguas that you can find at most botanicas and metaphysical stores are made from synthetic fragrances with little spiritual power. As Brujas we work with what we have around us, and there are many ways to energetically charge them. The following recipe is an "Agua Florida" (botanical/floral water) for cutting negative energetic ties and cords, clearing attachments, invoking and evoking Spirit to be present in the self and in your spaces in clear, calm, and collected ways, and cleansing the self before the altar.

Mediums, workers in *Espiritismo* or Latin Spiritualist traditions of the Americas, and those of us who do many public readings can become overwhelmed by the energetic material that can come with each client. As a way of breaking this energy, clearing it from the body and aura, and refreshing the self, this is an additional practice that can be added into our repertoires. Noon and midnight can be especially energetically intense, and Brujas often have versions of this agua on their ancestral altars to clean themselves during the day and during those time periods.

You can find these ingredients using the resource list in the back of the book and by contacting your local metaphysical stores or botanicas. Each ingredient carries a history and intended use, described below, and in this practice, you will be asked to speak aloud the respective prayers to invite the spirit of each ingredient into your practice.

5 store-bought aguas, like Florida, Vetiver, Rose, Lavender, Tobacco, Lotion Pompeia, or Kolonia 1800

basil

siguaraya

vencedor

rompe saraguey

yerba buena/mint

cascarilla

tobacco from ancestral altar

mason jar

Plant Medicines

Basil (*Ocimum basilicum*): Basil is indigenous to tropical regions ranging from central Africa to Southeast Asia. Its proliferation as a culinary herb, internal medicine, and magico-religious plant has spread worldwide. Basil is brought up several times throughout this book because of its importance and stature within these traditions. It acts as a medicinal and spiritual anti-inflammatory (removes heat and irritation) and is especially engaged with conditions such as peptic ulcers, irritable bowel syndrome, high cholesterol, and arthritis, and it supports blood sugar regulation and aids in supporting proper liver function and detoxifying the body. "Basil, Spirit that attracts all positive, Enlightened, and elevated energies and Beings, we call to you today to join us in this work. Basil, who promotes coolness and removes irritation, guide me toward cultivating this medicine. Show me ways to be empowered, to stay composed internally and in my responses in the world, and help me to de-escalate and defuse triggering situations. Basil, we call you to join our works."

Siguaraya (*Trichilia havanensis*): Native to Venezuela, Mexico, and the Caribbean, siguaraya is a helper both medicinally and magico-spiritually. Medicinally engaged for kidney support during the passing of kidney stones, it widens the restrictive flows, supports healthy joints and lessens rheumatic discomfort, assists in skin repair and scar healing, and treats sexually transmitted infections. Spiritually, siguaraya expels negativity that has been ingested or tries to nonconsensually attach itself to us or our spaces; it banishes internalized negative thoughts, curses, witchcrafts, and other maledictive forces. When planted near the boundaries of our properties, homes, businesses, and other places of importance, it guards and protects these spaces by creating strong energetic boundaries. "Spirit of Siguaraya, work with me to create protective boundaries where I can consent to the energies that are let in. Shine a spotlight on any intruders and expel them both internally and in all of my spaces. Help me to cut cords and banish all forces of dispossession. Strengthen and fortify my altar and create a fortress of protection."

Vencedor (*Zanthoxylum pistacifolium*): Indigenous to Caribbean and Gulf of Mexico regions of Central America, vencedor, when prepared under guidance, works with the nervous system, is antifungal, and eases menstrual cramping. Metaphysically, it is a controlling and dominating botanical that claims territory and space. It assists with cleansing and purification rites by helping the person claim their space and their power and moving all other energies out. It is known to attract positive influences and forces and can help overcome difficult situations. In combinations with other medicinal plants, it is known as a strong love herb that can help us claim the affection that we deserve. "Vencedor, walk with us in our work and be present in our ceremonies. Spirit of domination, control, and claiming our power, ally yourself with us as we stand in our strength and take control of any situation. We ask you to assist us in clearing away all negative entities, forces, and enemies, and help us attract love, compassion, understanding, and benevolent Spirits."

Rompe saraguey (*Eupatorium odoratum*): Native to South America, southern Mexico, Texas, Florida, and the Caribbean, rompe saraguey is a larvicide that kills all species of mosquitoes before they reach adulthood. It is also known as a wound healer, with several parts of the plant treating ailments from burns and infections, and it has anticancer, antidiabetic, anti-inflammatory, and antioxidant properties. Rompe saraguey strips and tears away layers of caked-on negative and past traumas that are carried in our physical, mental, and emotional memories and auras. It banishes negativity and exorcises unwanted and uninvited energetic guests and pests. "Rompe Saraguey, tear away past pains, traumas, and torments from ourselves and our environments and help us to start fresh. Spirit that strips away the things that haunt us, help us to banish addictions, behaviors, oppressive internal dialogues, negative people, entities, and forces that are unsupportive and wish us ill. Rompe Saraguey, guard us and those we love, and help us to expel all low-vibrating beings."

Yerba buena (*Clinopodium douglasii*): Yerba buena is a member of the mint family, and this specific variety is indigenous to the western United States, Canada, and Mexico, and is known to reach the coastal regions of Alaska. Medicinally engaged as a stomach and digestion assistant, mint has memory-supporting properties and improves symptoms of irritable bowel. Spiritually, yerba buena is known as a road opener, block buster, and good luck attractor. Much of these associations are rooted in how it grows in the wild as well as how it handles insects and pests. Ornamentally planted as a ground cover, it spreads and covers its territory, literally, choking out other botanicals in the area and claiming the space for itself. In Traditional Chinese Medicine it is known for having cooling properties and can expel spiritual heat that is absorbed in the body. "Yerba Buena, we call to you to assist us in our work, Spirit of Coolness, help us to recognize heat, chaos, and confusion in ourselves, our relationships, and our environments. Dispel it in all forms and support us in stepping out of reactionary modes and behaviors. Yerba Buena, herb that breaks through obstacles and opens the roads, help us to identify and remove them before they exist in the material world. Spirit of good fortune that spreads, support our nervous systems, cool our hearts, and spread luck and grace throughout our lives."

Tobacco from the ancestral altar: Tobacco will be spoken about in length later in this chapter, and its inclusion in this formula is a way of allowing your ancestral court, spirit, guides, and guardians, "those that walk with us," to be present in this work and supporting you at all times. Tobacco is also smoldered on incense charcoals in front of the altar at times both to lift up our prayers and to provide a cleansing fumigation. "Spirit of Tobacco, we call to all those Beings, Spirits, Guides, and Helpers who stand by us and support our elevation, evolution, and progress mentally, spiritually, physically, and emotionally. We ask that they be present in this work and aid us at all times. Spirit of Tobacco, we call you to be present."

Cascarilla: Made from the ground-up shells of white chicken eggs that are hollowed out and cleaned, cascarilla energetically mimics a bentonite clay compound found in southwestern Nigeria and the Democratic Republic of the Congo. Representing the purity of our Spirits and our connections to the Source and the Creator, cascarilla is engaged to physically draw down divinities and create boundaries and energetic fences that negative entities cannot cross. Cascarilla has a long history in religious rites and initiations in Afro-diasporic traditions in the Americas. "Spirit of Cascarilla, Spirit of Purity, Blessings, and Grace, assist us in demarcating our boundaries both internally and within our relationships and homes, and support our connections with the Source and Creator."

Procedure

After all the ingredients have been blessed and consecrated and sacred space has been created, you will first start with the plant and zoological medicines. As you call to each plant and ask it to be with you in the work, you will exhale forcefully three times on the material and visualize your life force going into the botanicals and bringing them to life. Once you have finished with these steps, add the combination of at least five spiritual waters that you can find at any botanica or metaphysical store. Remember that it's not about equal portions of things and in formulation, it's about the quality and purpose of creation. The next section contains a list of some common spiritual waters and their purposes. The final step is to say your intent of how you want the whole mixture to come alive and what its goal or purpose is and breathe three times into the jar. Sometimes practitioners take the additional step of either blowing or directing cigar/tobacco smoke into the jar as they seal and close it. This spiritual water is left on the altar to charge. It repels negative spirits just by being on the altar and can be used to clean the self and others.

Aguas

Agua Florida: Overall blessing, cooling, cleansing water.

Agua de Sandalo: Spiritually lifts, elevates, and attracts enlightened beings.

Kolonia 1800: Cleanses, clears, and removes negative energies.

Kolonia 1800 Vetiver: Breaks and tears away negative entities and attracts good luck.

Agua de Rosas: Blesses, uplifts, and attracts divinities and higher teachers.

Agua de Violetas: Compassion, beauty, grace, elegance, sweetness, innocence.

Lotion Pompeia: Fortune, beauty, seduction, power, charm, charisma, money, prosperity.

Kolonia 1800 Tobacco: Lifting our prayers to the Creator, honoring medicine, clearing, guarding, and protection.

Agua Florida, North American 1808–1830 Recipe(s)

As mentioned, even in the 1830s when it originated, Florida Water had several versions and derivations. Over the last couple of decades, I've researched recipes and put together an amalgamation of most of the popular ingredients. These formulas are predominantly top- and heart-note heavy (I will explain more in chapter 5) with little to no base-note depth. None of the manufactured Agua Florida fragrances available now would in any way smell similar to these originals.

12 citrons, grated

6 bergamot oranges, grated

4 cups orange blossoms

3 cups lime blossoms

2 cups lemon blossoms

3 cups citrus petitgrain (combination of bark, leaves, and buds)

¼ cup cloves

⅛ cup cinnamon bark

5 cups fresh rose petals

5 cups fresh jasmine blossoms

3 tablespoons lavender blossoms

1 gallon 180 proof alcohol

1 gallon glass mason jar

grater

large glass bowl

Please note that once you have made the base tincture it will sit for six weeks, and then you will be exploring scenting that mixture with essential oils, as listed in the next part of the recipe. You may want to use that time to gather the materials needed for the next step if you do not have them yet.

Foundation: Creating a Perfumer's Tincture

Tincturing in scent and fragrance development is the process through which a plant's natural oils and medicinal constituents are extracted using alcohol. I use 180 proof organic grain alcohol, but in a pinch you can use Everclear or 100 proof rubbing alcohol. I do not advise using vodka, gin, rum, or any other alcoholic spirit under 100 proof because they do not have the levels needed to pull out most of the plant material or carry the scent.

1. Follow the initial steps given in the first chapter (page 16).

2. As you move from honoring and imbuing all the tools with intent, you will continue this process with the herbs, oils, and alcohol using the smudge only. Sometimes I might lightly mist the fresh herbal material with water, but I personally stay away from alcohol because it will wilt the plant (alcohol literally pushes water out of the cell; that is part of the reason we feel hung over when we drink).

3. Now to get things rolling. Grab the bowl, grater, and citrons. When grating any fruit skins for medicine, remember to stop before you reach the pith of the fruit (the white coating on the underside of the skin). The pith is deeply bitter and acidic and can ruin a great tincture. Some people use vegetable peelers instead of grating, but that method takes longer for the alcohol to extract the essences. If your grater has multiple size options, start small.

4. After you have finished grating, gather your energy and imagine it flowing into the peel. When you are ready, speak to the citron about the ways it can aid you in the work. I extemporaneously follow my heart, but as an example you could say something like, "Citron, Spirit that sweetens our paths, attracts our blessings, essence of grace and beauty, open my roads and senses to the possibilities around me. Spirit that cuts negativity, assist me in recognizing negativity before it manifests in my life and tear away anything that is not uplifting." Next, gently breathe into the peel three times, giving it the breath of life and its charge in the formula, and add it to the jar.

5. The next ingredient is the **bergamot oranges**. Bergamot, one of the constituents of Earl Grey tea, is native to southern Italy. It has less of a sour taste and smell than lemons and limes but is more bitter than grapefruit. Spiritually, bergamot is a protector plant specifically aiding to stay juicy despite heated and arid conditions; it balances and assists in prioritizing what is really important in our lives, promotes joy, and builds esteem and confidence. As it is also in the citrus family, it is another road-opening ingredient.

Just like you did with the citrons, grate the bergamot. Don't forget to stay away from the pith!

When you are ready, align the bergamot with its purpose. Your flow from now on is as follows, and with each ingredient you will align it with a specific intent. First, it's time to build up the energy; then speak your intent; next, gently breathe on it three times, bringing it to life; and finally, add it to the jar. For bergamot you want to draw out the joyous, esteem-building properties of the fruit. An example you can build off of could be, "Bergamot, fruit of joy, help me to be joyous in every second of my life. Assist me in recognizing the places where I have accepted suffering, and help me to liberate myself into enjoyment. Bergamot, Protector Spirit, shield me from heat and teach me how to stay juicy in the most arid of environments. I call upon you, Bergamot, to support me as I affirm my worth, importance, and value in my life."

6. Next, move to the **orange blossoms**—if you want to be technical, specifically from the bitter orange tree (if you live near citrus farms or commercial nurseries, give them a call because you can get great deals on blossoms and damaged fruits). Neroli oil is distilled from orange blossoms, whereas orange oil is extracted from the skin. Oranges, native to southern China, northeastern India, and Myanmar, have migrated across the globe and are one the world's most recognizable fruits. Orange blossom and neroli oil are mood elevators and stabilizers and can assist with depression, fatigue, and isolation and help to soothe the nervous system after we are triggered.

Orange blossoms turn brown extremely fast and must be used within an hour after picking. Separate the petals from the stems and other plant material, and remove any diseased or brown petals. When you are ready, just like you did with the citrons and bergamot, you are going to align the orange blossoms with their purpose. Just as above, first build up the energy; then speak the intent; next, gently breathe on it three times, bringing it to life; and finally, add it to the jar. Your sample intention could be, "Orange Blossoms, energies that uplift the heaviest of hearts and despair, pierce through the fogs and elevate my burdens. Spirit of Orange Blossoms, help to calm anxieties, ease stress, and cool my nervous system."

7. Lime (*Citrus latifolia*) originates from Myanmar and Malaysia, and its blossoms are connected to clearing away obstacles, blocks, and the spiritual detritus that is accumulated from absorbing other people's moods and thoughts. Lime's acidic nature helps give courage and strength to those feeling apathetic, passionless, weighed down by grief, and hopeless that things can change.

Following the same methodology as with the orange blossoms, separate the petals, remove any browning or diseased material, and energize them. "Lime Blossoms, I come to you today to cut away all blockages, burst all energetic dams, and peel anything that has been absorbed that is not of my highest good." Breathe three times and add to jar.

8. Lemon (*Citrus limon*) is a fruit native to South Asia and is one of the more astringent citruses. The blossoms have a narcotic floral aroma with lemon undertones, and this scent can permeate a room with just a few flowers left in a bowl of water. Lemon blossoms are natural purifiers—they lift out everything that is not of us, and they support us through transformational processes as we change from one state of being to the next. Lemon aids in healing unbalanced attachment difficulties, it supports action-orientated behaviors by moving from process into problem-solving strategies, and it represents longevity and clarity. "Spirit of New Beginnings, help me to clear away all that is no longer my highest good. I purify myself of all attachments that may throw me off my center. Spirit of Lemon, support my healing processes as I transform and elevate." Breathe three times and add to jar.

9. Petitgrain (*Citrus aurantium ssp. amara*) is derived from all the constituent parts of the bitter orange tree (but I have used any citrus tree I can get my hands on)—the leaves, bark, and flowers. Each element has its function—the bark is the protective skin of the plant, the leaves are the location of energy created through photosynthesis, and the blossoms are the sites of reproduction—and together they hold the totality of the tree's being. As you work with the petitgrain, notice that each part has a different element of citrus fragrance: the wood brings out the deeper citrus tones but is faint. The leaves have a greener smell (like freshly mown lawn combined with citrus). The blossoms have the sweeter, floral top notes. Petitgrain is used to relieve stress and anxiety. It promotes relaxation and illuminates places of mental claustrophobia while giving us tools to break through those constraints. "Spirit of Petitgrain, shine light on the places where I am selling myself short, illuminate my worth and assist me in breaking through these shortcomings. Petitgrain, help me to notice my stress and anxiety and guide me toward ease and help to see where labor is actually needed." Breathe three times and add to jar.

10. Cloves are the dried flower buds of *Syzygium aromaticum*, a tree originally from the Maluku Islands in Indonesia. Promoting self-love, platonic love, and romantic love, clove moves us toward action and adds vitality. Another aspect of this plant is its luck and ease, properties said to advocate for us through offering insights on how and where to place one's attention and energy, as well as being prepared for the opportunity to arrive at any time. One of the last aspects of clove is its protective nature. Medicinally, clove can cause irritation and can burn the skin if used without dilution, and spiritually its energies can be harnessed in the same manner (burning away slander, gossip, and negative statements made by others). "Spirit of Clove, help me to prepare myself for the opportunities I seek and guide me toward the blessings that are already arriving. Clove, I ask you to fortify my resolve and assist me in having the courage to seek connection and love in its many faces and forms. Help me to be vulnerable with those who can show kindness and vulnerability in return and reveal those who do not have my interests at heart." Breathe three times and add to jar.

11. Cinnamon (*Cinnamomum verum* and *Cinnamomum zeylanicum Blume*) is indigenous to the Malabar region of India and Sri Lanka. Representing luck, fortune, prosperity, speed, drive, and attraction, cinnamon has a fast-acting nature. It is similar to clove in its irritating properties; if the undiluted oil comes into contact with any mucus membranes, it will burn like crazy (trust me, I know). Both clove and cinnamon can overwhelm and overpower a fragrance, so they should always be used sparingly. "Cinnamon, Spirit of drive, passion, attraction, and fortune, align me with luck and assist me to be deliberate, unified, and quick to move toward my fortunes." Breathe three times and add to jar.

12. Roses are found in most areas of the world and are some of the highest-vibrating flowers on the planet. Rose is the queen of perfumery and can spotlight aspects of other flowers. Spiritually, rose softens the heart and allows us to authentically express ourselves and our desires without judgment. Rose is also a symbol of love and mutual affirmation and can help express the feelings of the heart. "Spirit of Rose, essence of affection, grace, and beauty, walk with me on my path toward blooming. Help me to soften my heart to affirmation and understanding, and teach me the ways of compassion both for myself and all those around me. I ask you, Rose, to come forth and be an ally in this work." Breathe three times and add to jar.

13. Jasmine (genus *Jasminum*) has an origin in Eurasia, Australasia, and Oceania and has been introduced through most subtropical regions of the globe. In Brujería it is symbolic of love on a spiritual level, and it allows us to recognize beings of similar energy. It is also called upon to aid in astral (perception beyond vision) and dream workings. In spiritual perfumery it is considered another fundamental flower, like rose, that brings warmth and highlights the qualities of other scents. "Jasmine, Spirit of perception beyond our senses, help me to be aware in all ways. Open up my mind's eye with gentle protection so I can perceive and communicate with those higher Beings around me. Help me to dream of those who are Transcendent Ancestors and support me to be aware of Beings who are negative. Jasmine, come into my life and guide me toward those who have genuine love and affection." Breathe three times and add to jar.

14. Lavender (genus *Lavandula* with numerous species), indigenous to the western Mediterranean region of Europe, has both medicinal and spiritual properties. Medicinally, lavender helps to calm the nerves, soothes low-grade chemical burns, and supports restfulness and sleep. Spiritually, it promotes peace and resolution to conflict, helps to soothe stressors and irritations (takes the burn out), and cools anger. In perfumery it can be another overwhelming scent that takes things in a menthol direction. For our purposes we are engaging it only in the petal form in this recipe. "Lavender, Spirit who calms and soothes, help me to engage stress in a new way. Help me to cool tensions and conflicts, remove all irritants and inflammatory presences, and attract happiness, joy, and love into my life. Lavender, I call to you this day to bring in peace and restfulness and help me to truly sleep well and with ease." Breathe three times and add to jar.

15. Now you are at the stage of adding alcohol. As I pour, I usually offer a simple intention into the alcohol, asking that it act as a medium for extracting all the medicines, intentions, and Spirits of each plant and harmonize them together to act as one. After everything is fully integrated into the mixture, I say a final intention over the whole thing before I seal it up. "I call to all the flowers, fruits, and plants held here, and I ask that you uplift, sweeten, cleanse, and open all roads before me. Elevate my heart and bring joy into my life as I walk with protection, awareness, and peace throughout my days." Breathe three times and add to jar. Seal the jar.

16. Once the jar is sealed, the magics are complete. You can now release the energies and ground the space. I like to start by thanking all the Spirits that have been called on with something simple like, "Thank you for your assistance and continuing to walk with me. I ground your lessons and medicines in my work, heart, and body and leave in peace." At this point clap or ring a bell to open the space and release the energies that have been called. Now you can move about and clean up.

Sit and Strain

Let this mixture sit for 4 to 6 weeks in a cool, dark place away from any fire sources. Every day during this time, come back to your jar and swish everything around while saying a universal intent of what you would like this mixture to do on your behalf. Over time the mixture will turn a deep green, and you will notice the peels, petals, and bark starting to whiten as all the medicines are extracted. After about 6 weeks it will be time to strain the liquid from the plant materials. After straining, the plant materials can be thanked for their assistance and composted.

Please note that natural Agua Florida has a shelf life of about 9 to 10 months before the citrus notes start to fade and the original sparkle of the tincture dulls. Adding your fragrance on top helps to add dimension and give it greater longevity, tenacity, and throw.

Also note that you don't have to go through the microcosmic orbit or libation every time you swirl the jar, but these practices help in the process, especially for foundational practice; we have to start somewhere.

Brujería Lab: Scenting Experimentation

Now that you have a magically scented alcohol base that has been enchanted with the intentions, you will move to the next step, scenting! This part of the process is the cherry on top of the sundae; it is a way to explore and to personalize the scent, to really make it your own based on the wisdom of your own senses. You will need the following ingredients and items:

bergamot essential oil   **rose essential oil**

neroli essential oil   **lime essential oil**

jasmine essential oil	7 droppers or pipettes
clove essential oil	rubbing alcohol and cup
cinnamon essential oil	watercolor paper cut
3 or 4 small (0.5 ounce) glass bottles	into 2-inch strips
	journal
measuring beaker (15–20 ml in size)	

1. Gather your oils, tincturing base, measuring beaker, bottles, pipettes, watercolor paper, and rubbing alcohol with a cup.

2. Pour a generous amount of rubbing alcohol into the cup; this will be used to clean the pipettes once you are finished with them. Set aside the pieces of watercolor paper as well because they will be used as test strips for the experimentation process.

3. You will be creating different versions of the scent, so that's why you start off small. Pour 5 ml of the base tincture into the beaker; now you are ready to experiment. Perfumery starts with the base notes (the longest-lasting oils that stay on the skin), proceeding to the heart notes or juice of the scent, concluding with the top notes, which are usually smelled first in the fragrance profile but are the shortest-lasting fragrance.

4. From the list above, cinnamon and clove are the base notes (sometimes perfumers classify them as heart and top notes depending on how they are used and the forms of extractions), but remember that in large quantities they can overwhelm and irritate the skin. Consider using 1 drop of each to start. Now dip a piece of the test strip into the potion and let it dry. Consider adding 1 drop to your skin and letting it dry. Smell both the test strip and your skin and record your impressions. Is it warm, spicy, bitter? Where does it fall on your palate? How long does it last on your skin and on the strip?

5. The heart notes on the list are rose, jasmine, and neroli. Neroli is going to be the star in this combo, so start off with 5 drops neroli, 2 drops rose, and 1 drop jasmine. As above, test on a paper strip and a different area of your skin, and record your findings.

6. Finally, the top notes, lime and bergamot, come into play. Too many citruses compete against each other and can cause everything to go cloudy and lose their distinctiveness (think of all those generic "citrus" fragrances that are out there). Lime especially can be a bit harsh. Consider diluting the lime by taking one of your extra bottles, adding 1–2 drops of the oil, and filling the rest up with alcohol. From this dilution take 1–2 drops and add it to the perfume experiment. Next, take a drop or two of bergamot and add it as the final ingredient. Using your pipette as a stirrer, mix things up and swish them around gently. As above, take a drop and add it to your skin and test strips and record your results.

7. Decant this into one of your bottles and set aside for two weeks. After it has rested for the desired amount of time, record your impressions: What does it need, what would you like to try next, and so on.

8. Create your own recipes with the tincture base and have a blast! For information on how to scale up the recipe, see chapter 5.

Peruvian-Inspired Agua Florida Recipe

This version of Agua Florida is inspired by traditional Peruvian recipes, and I have made revisions based on the availability of the herbs outside of South America. One of its many distinctions is that it smells sweeter than the original, and while it still has some of the same cleansing and cooling properties, the emphasis has moved toward affection, love, ease in transitions, and astral communication. Part of

Brujería is that the magics respond to the conditions of their people as well as what is available in the practitioners' bioregions.

rosa cisa (*Tagetes erecta*) blossoms

labios de novia (*Psychotria poeppigiana*) blossoms

chiric sanango (*Brunfelsia grandiflora*)[4]

piri-piri (*Cyperus articulatus L.*)

orange blossoms

orange peel

rose blossoms

vanilla pod

180 proof sugarcane alcohol

Oils for Scent Lab:

orange blossom oil

rose oil

petitgrain oil

cinnamon oil

You will follow the same process that is listed on page 35, and below you can discover the ingredients we haven't used as well as their smells and energetic qualities.

Ingredient Highlights

1. Rosa cisa (*Tagetes erecta*) is a type of common marigold native to Central America. This plant in all its varieties has had a central place in Brujería medicine making and ceremony since before conquest. Rosa cisa or marigold has spread across the Americas and Caribbean because of its deep commitment to helping people. Connected to solar energy and renewal, the marigold symbolizes the illumination of the Creator mirrored within the soul, soul-fire/soul-sun, the emanating breath of life that is present even in death. Medicinally, it has been engaged to treat various internal ailments, such as indigestion

---

4   Usually the leaves and other plant material are utilized, but in this recipe blossoms are utilized.

and constipation, as well as external conditions such as eczema, ulcers, and sores. Spiritually, it promotes security and nurturing during change and transitions, even the most dramatic changes, such as death and rebirth. Rosa cisa speaks to the ancestral voices and wisdoms held within each cell and the ability to tap into those powers. "Rosa cisa, I call to you to help me sit in the transcendent ancestral wisdom. Spirit of transcendence, transformation, and the rebirth of the soul, I ask you to be present." Breathe three times and add to jar.

2. Labios de novia (*Psychotria poeppigiana*) is distributed throughout South and Central America, and its blossoms literally look like huge red lips. Made into a strong tea, labios de novia medicinally treats bruises, sprains, rheumatism, and headaches. Depending on the part of the plant that is harvested, it can treat everything from whooping cough to earaches. Spiritually, it is connected to deep inner affirmation and self-love as well as having those around us speak lovingly to us. This plant kisses the world and draws kisses to us. "Labios de Novia, help me to deeply kiss and embrace the parts of myself that I try to hold. Help me to fall in love with myself and to reflect those qualities in all my interactions. I ask you to kiss me, kiss this water, and kiss my beloveds with grace, beauty, tenderness, and sweetness." Breathe three times and add to jar.

3. Chiric sanango (*Brunfelsia grandiflora*) is an extremely hallucinogenic and toxic plant, and I will not be addressing how to engage it here. The only way I suggest having a relationship with it outside of a qualified Elder in *mesa* practices of Peru would be in homeopathic plant essence form.

4. Piri-piri (*Cyperus articulatus L.*) is a plant in relationship with the peoples throughout the Amazon. In Peru it is used medicinally with issues surrounding contraception, childbirth, and digestive issues. In the Guianas, piri-piri is used to reduce fevers, induce sweating, and as a treatment for chronic diarrhea. Spiritually, piri-piri is linked to astral travel or the ability of the consciousness to move beyond the body, and it is a healer plant connecting our communication to our most elevated helpers. "Piri-Piri, helper plant and Spirit that aids us in connecting ourselves to our Guides, walk with me and be present. I call to you to help me open myself to the vastness and outrageousness of my Being. Help me to allow myself to be truly as big as who I am. Walk with me as a protector plant as I journey beyond my physical self and guide me toward poignant experiences with Enlightened forces." Breathe three times and add to jar.

5. Vanilla is a spice derived from the seed pods of *Vanilla pompona* and *Vanilla planifolia*, which are indigenous species of the vanilla orchids found throughout the Amazon of Peru, northern South America, and southern Central America. Medicinally, vanilla is engaged for digestive care and as a natural sugar-free sweetener. Spiritually, vanilla has a sedative nature and is known to help relax the nervous system while maintaining focus and attention. Vanilla is a natural emotional pick-me-up, and it helps create empathy and understanding. "Vanilla, help me to sit in understanding of myself and any messages communicated for my highest good. Spirit of sweetness and empathy, help me to feel any places where I have numbed out, and guide me toward real, connected empathy for myself and those that I love." Breathe three times and add to jar.

Scent Distinctions

Both the sugarcane alcohol and the vanilla add the extra sweetness and depth and bring the orange forward in the scent, more so than the previous recipe. You may consider using this as a base perfume and researching Peruvian perfumery. What types of floral accords (harmonies between scents) are being produced? How can you stay authentic to the region and create an inspired recipe?

Lou's Agua Florida (All-Purpose)

My Agua Florida sneaks up on you with its sweet, seductive scent but will energetically clear out anything attached to or haunting you. It's one of a spectrum of formulas I use to break, cut, and tear entities off people and clear spaces.

citruses of all kinds	**pericón**
rose petals	**apazote**
cinnamon	**caimito**
clove	**prodigiosa**
cardamom	**bay laurel**
basil	**180 proof alcohol**

Oils for Scent Lab:

pink peppercorn essential oil	**jasmine essential oil**
bergamot essential oil	**sandalwood essential oil**
citron essential oil	**cardamom essential oil**
mimosa essential oil	**frankincense essential oil**

Ingredient Highlights

1. Any and all citruses are usable here. Grate the peels and avoid the pith. This gives the tincture an overall citrus-forward scent, and the essential oils will bring out the star citrus in the recipe, citron. Continue to work intentions listed under orange blossoms, bergamot, and other citruses in the two previous Agua Florida recipes, breathe on it three times, and add to your jar.

2. Cardamom (*Elettaria cardamomum*), native to Indonesia and the Indian subcontinent, is in the same family as ginger and Guinea pepper. Medicinally, cardamom assists with liver and gallbladder imbalances, intestinal gas, heartburn, and irritable bowl. Spiritually, it creates pathways for aligning oneself with new perspectives and experiences with passion, love, and inner sexuality and its expressions. Energetically, cardamom warms the system up, and vibrationally, it does the same. "Cardamom, Spirit of warmth and connectedness, help me share my warmth, generosity, and joy with the world; as we are in the right relationship, so are my relationships warm and generous. Spirit of passion, embodied sexuality, and pleasure, stand with me in this work." Breathe three times and add to jar.

3. Basil (*Ocimum basilicum*) is brought up several times throughout the book because of its importance and stature within these traditions. It acts as a medicinal and spiritual anti-inflammatory (removes heat and irritation) and is especially engaged with conditions such as peptic ulcers, irritable bowel syndrome, high cholesterol, and arthritis. It also supports blood sugar regulation and aids in supporting proper liver function and detoxifying the body. "Basil, Spirit that attracts all positive, Enlightened, and elevated energies and Beings, we call to you today to join us in this work. Basil, she who promotes coolness and removes irritation, guide me toward cultivating this medicine. Show me ways to be empowered, to stay composed internally and in my responses in the world, and help me to de-escalate and defuse triggering situations. Basil, we call to you to join our working." Breathe three times and add to jar.

4. Pericón (*Tagetes erecta*), in Brujería, is considered the grandmother plant of all marigold species and varieties. Native to Central America, the plant has significant cultural, medicinal, and spiritual properties, and its leaves have scent aspects of mint, anise, and tarragon. Classified as a warming herb that treats excess cold and dampness in the body from an Aztec perspective, pericón supports ease in childbirth and treats edema, tonsillitis, and sore throats. Spiritually, it has deep connections to Tlaloc, the divine emanation of rain and the water cycle itself. Pericón is a natural detoxifier and helps to elevate the consciousness by removing all the burdens and weight of everything that we have absorbed. As a Spirit connected with ancestral veneration and the cycles of rebirth and reincarnation, pericón awakens elevated ancestral Spirits and guides them on a river of light and memory into our lives. "Pericón, Grandmother Spirit who calls the Ancestors with her medicine, walk with us today. Spirit of Ancestral knowledge, guide us toward the wisdoms buried deep within. Enable us to sense, perceive, and balance the heat and cold within. Pericón, join us in this medicine." Breathe three times and add to jar.

5. Apazote (*Dysphania ambrosioides*) is native to South and Central America and southern Mexico; its name is etymologically rooted in the Nahuatl words *epatl* (skunk) and *tzotl* (the process that makes things perspire, get dingy, dirty, and grimy). Medicinally engaged to work with toothaches, menstrual cramping, intestinal parasites, malaria, and hypertension, apazote is a preconquest herb that continues to flourish and work with its peoples. Magically, apazote is a curse and hex breaker (not just the ideas of "spells" being put on us but all the limitations and narratives that we put on ourselves and others put on us). It's also an antiparasitic, meaning it is a good herb when dealing with cord cutting as well as psychic vampires. I've found it at most grocery stores and especially those specializing in Asian and

Central and South American and Caribbean foods. "Apazote, join us in this work and stand with us an ally. Help us to identify energetic connections and cords that are unhealthy and diseased as well as how to cut through them. Break narratives and attachments that are constrictive and binding, and liberate us toward fully being our largest, most authentic selves. Apazote, Spirit that destroys all parasites, remove any named and unnamed, any seen or unseen influences and beings that seek to harm or suck out my juiciness. Apazote, be present here in this medicine."

Note: Apazote is not recommended for those who are pregnant or breastfeeding.

6. Caimito (*Chrysophyllum cainito*) is the star apple tree, indigenous to the West Indies. Its mucilaginous properties have healing effects for those affected by pneumonia and laryngitis, and it is used to support oral health and hygiene, for wound healing, and as an antioxidant and digestive aid. Spiritually, caimito is used for sweeping up negative energies, situations, and messes. In many homes you can find its branches gathered into a bundle as a broom at the front door to ensure that nothing follows you through the threshold. "Caimito, Star Apple, Spirit that gathers and sweeps away all negating forces, help me to gather up all negative and self-defeating energies and sweep them out of our lives. Physically, mentally, emotionally, and spiritually, wherever those energies may reside, remove them this day from ourselves and our environments, Spirit of Caimito, join us in our work."

7. Prodigiosa (*Kalanchoe daigremontiana*) is a succulent originally from Madagascar; in Spanish it is known as siempre viva and prodigiosa (both names speaking to the thriving nature and energy of the plant). It is also known as "mother of thousands" for its ability to propagate multiple plants from one leaf. Medicinally, prodigiosa is used to treat burns, infections, ulcers, vomiting, stroke, and cough. Prodigiosa is a helper plant that finds usefulness by positively interacting with its environment. Known spiritually as a botanical that can reawaken numbness and loss of feeling, it is a holy plant that aligns us to thriving and regeneration. "Prodigiosa, Holy emissary that replenishes, revives, and resurrects, support my inner regeneration and help reawaken all those places where I have gone numb and lost feeling. Like the blood that courses through our bodies, course through my body like a luminous wave to bring life, vitality, and blessings from the inside out." Breathe three times and add to jar.

8. Bay laurel (*Laurus nobilis*) is native to Turkey, Syria, North Africa, and the Mediterranean region and has been a cultural reference since antiquity. Grown as a culinary spice, bay laurel is often called upon as an analgesic (treats pain), and it can treat the flu, bronchitis, and migraines. Its spiritual associations range from authority, prestige, honor, and acknowledgment to miracle working, spontaneous healing, and divination. Bay laurel is known as a spiritual truth teller, and it can bring to light all that is hidden. "Bay Laurel, Miracle Maker, Truth Teller, support us as we seek the truth in all situations, and help us to feel empowered and courageous as we stand in our Divine Warriorhood. Spirit of prestige and blessings, come forth and share your medicine." Breathe three times and add to jar.

Scent Distinctions

1. Base Notes: Frankincense, cardamom, and sandalwood.

Frankincense is one of the only base fragrances that has citrus notes as part of its scent, and this adds a longer-lasting, well-rounded kiss of citrus to the mixture. I would play with a more sandalwood-dominant proportion of drops with the cardamom and frankincense as accents.

Sandalwood (*Santalum album*) is native to India, Indonesia, and Australia, with the most notable variety being the Indian. Sandalwood's root structures are similar to aspen's in that they are all interconnected and part of one larger root mother with its trees appearing separate above ground. The awe-inspiring nature of this root matrix is phenomenal in that all the trees in the forest sense, perceive, and act as one. The impact of climate change and commercial demand for sandalwood has decimated ancient forests and has nearly driven it to the point of extinction. To avoid contributing to the extinction of the East Indian sandalwood tree, look for sandalwood oil that has been sustainably sourced from Laos, Thailand, Vietnam, or Australia.

Medicinally, sandalwood is an antiseptic and astringent, and supports acne treatments, urinary imbalances, and headaches. Spiritually speaking, sandalwood is one of the highest-vibrational trees on the planet. It speaks to divine transmissions and communications, evolution, clarity, calming, peacefulness, and meditative introspection. Sandalwood is categorized as a sweetening consciousness, and it elevates, refreshes, and brings joy to everything in its environment. "Spirit of Sandalwood, Being that inspires authentic Enlightenment and fulfillment of our true purpose and Will, work with us today to elevate and liberate ourselves and the generations to come. Be present as advocate and ally to support our advancements."

Frankincense (*Boswellia sacra*) comes from a variety of trees from the Burseraceae family and is a native of Yemen, Oman, and the Horn of Africa. Frankincense's curative properties have been known throughout history; it is medicinally engaged as an antiseptic for wound healing, analgesic, expectorant, and anti-inflammatory. In magical practice, frankincense is similar to sandalwood in its ability to elevate and sweeten. It is called on to invoke and evoke high-vibrational consciousness, divinities, and Spirit into ourselves and our spaces. Due to its citrus/menthol undertones, it can cut negative energies and clear stagnancy. "Frankincense, Spirit and messenger of Divinities, be with us in our work. Work through our bodies, minds, and Spirits to remind us of our divine sparks, and cut away all lower energies, situations, and people."

2. Heart Notes: Jasmine, mimosa, and citron.

The star fragrance of this formula is the citron, which has a lemony, Fruity-Pebbles-breakfast-cereal scent profile. The mimosa by itself has a soft, almost indistinct floral throw that moves to a powdery smell and highlights and smooths out other flowers within the accord. The jasmine is secondary to the citron and adds a honeyed roundness to the citrus tones.

Mimosa (*Acacia dealbata*) is a relative of beans and peanuts (the Fabaceae family) and is native to Tasmania and southeastern Australia. Medically, it is known to support wound care, pain relief, and the treatment of internal bleeding, dysentery, and hemorrhoids. Spiritually, mimosa represents secret desires that we wish to fulfill and crushes that we wish to follow. Mimosa aids us in opening up our sensitivities as well as in understanding the messages received. It is connected to expansion and potentiality and dreaming bigger for ourselves than we could possibly believe. "Mimosa, Spirit of expansion and desire, help us to admit and articulate the life we truly wish to live. Support us as we investigate these possibilities, and aid us in hearing our divine purpose."

3. Top Notes: Pink peppercorn and bergamot.

The top notes are pink peppercorn–forward, the bergamot adding a little bit of sparkle and pizzazz without needing to announce itself. The peppercorn is both spicy and floral, giving the scent a little kick, but it fades to the citron and jasmine in the heart notes and eventually fades to the frankincense and sandalwood to complete the throw.

Pink peppercorn (*Schinus molle*), native to Peru, is medicinally known as an antiseptic and diuretic and has disinfectant properties. Spiritually known to support courage and action-oriented behaviors, it energizes and protects while promoting honesty in communication and the heart. "Pink Peppercorn, help me to take action and prioritize the things that will move my life forward. Help me to be deliberate with my energies, and help me to speak up for the things that are important and valuable in my life. Pink Peppercorn, be with us in this work." Breathe three times and add to jar.

Agua Florida for Cleaning the Altar and Clearing Spaces

While the all-purpose recipe mentioned previously is a bit more forceful when it comes to its cleansing and exorcising properties, this recipe is no joke either. It clears on an intention and prayer level, clears sites of tragedies and loss, and rebalances our auric fields.

fresh citrus (anything in the orange/lemon family)	jasmine
	rose
bay leaf	rue
cloves	purple basil
cinnamon	lemongrass
fennel	camphor (just a pinch)

grains of paradise/Guinea
pepper/melegueta pepper/
alligator pepper

pericón

brugmansia/floripondio
plant essence

nicotiana/tobacco

sage

rose

180 proof alcohol

Oils for Scent Lab:

bergamot oil

pink peppercorn oil

neroli oil

ylang-ylang oil

jasmine oil

sandalwood oil

labdanum oil

benzoin oil

Ingredient Highlights

1. Fennel (*Foeniculum vulgare*) is a culinary herb with medicinal and spiritual properties that is native to southern Europe, the Mediterranean, and Turkey. As a culinary and medicinal herb, it assists in digestion (especially of heavy meals) and is a carminative (herb that releases gas and bloating) and a natural appetite suppressant; it stimulates recall and memory; and it has antispasmodic, anti-inflammatory, and antioxidant properties. Spiritually, fennel is a spiritual antiparasitic and one of the ingredients commonly associated with removing the evil eye. It is a great reversing herb in that it helps "vomit up" anything poisonous and send it back to its origination and also reduces the "heat" of jealousy and envy. "Spirit of Fennel, assist us in this work. Bring awareness to places where I am 'overheated,' and assist me in being in balance. Protective Spirit who supports me in identifying people, situations, and environments that are not of my highest good, walk with me as a shield and guardian, and help me to stand in the courage and strength that is needed to persevere." Breathe three times and add to jar.

2. Rue, ruda (*Ruta graveolens*), is a strong-scented plant (in different varieties it can smell like diesel fuel) that is native to Eurasia and the Canary Islands. Rue has huge influence in Brujería; the male sex of the species is connected to financial luck, gains in fortune, and victory in employment matters, while the female sex of the species is related to protection and reversing of negativity and is an anti-maledictive (neutralizes curses, jinxes, and domination workings, particularly things said from the tongue or negative gazes). Rue is a great ally for those elevating from a negative self-image and self-talk. "Ruda, Spirit that fights for and elevates its peoples, be present here and lend us support. Aid us in neutralizing all negative thoughts, ill wishes, and jealousies, either internal or in our environment. Help us to uproot and reverse all oppressions, said or unsaid, and attract to us all the fortunes and luck in the creation." Breathe three times and add to jar.

3. Purple basil, *Ocimum basilicum*, and basils of all variations are another extremely common botanical in Brujería. Native to various tropical regions, including in Africa and Southeast Asia, basil is a prominent culinary and spiritual herb known globally. As a medicinal, basil is known to promote blood circulation after childbirth, is an antispasmodic and a carminative (relieves gas), supports proper kidney function, and has anthelmintic (worm treating) properties. On a spiritual level, basil tears away negative witchcraft and maledictive energies and consciousnesses while attracting affirmative/positive influences, beings, and Spirits. Basil is also associated with money and financial workings. "Basil, we call you into our work to support our efforts to shed all layers of negativity and ill intentions from all sources, both internal and external, as well as those things that have been absorbed through contact. Spirit of positivity that attracts the most enlightened and elevated forces, help me to rise in my own illumination and affirm my power in newer and more poignant forms."

4. Lemongrass (*Cymbopogon schoenanthus*) and the *Cymbopogon* genus of grasses are indigenous to the tropical regions of Africa, Asia, and Australia. Its name is associated with lemons because of its scent. Lemongrass is made into a tea with other botanicals to treat anxiety, and its medicinal qualities include supporting erythropoiesis (creation of red blood cells), promoting blood pressure health, and reducing intestinal cramping; it is also known as an antiepileptic and disinfectant, and it is one of the main ingredients of insect repellents. Spiritually, lemongrass is associated with breaking through obstacles, promoting vitality and energy within workings, and repelling people and situations that are "bugging" you, and it is engaged to turn bad luck into good. (Interesting fact: lemongrass mimics the pheromone of a honeybee's Nasonov gland, which signals the bees to swarm or return to their hive. A true master of discernment!) "Spirit of Lemongrass, master of vitality, strength, and power, support our efforts and align us in our power in every moment of our lives. We call to you to assist in recognizing obstacles and breaking through them with ease and grace. Lemongrass, repel all 'bugs,' whether spiritual, mental, emotional, or physical, and help us to identify and repel those people and forces who need to exit our lives." Breathe three times and add to jar.

5. Camphor (you only need a pinch!) is a resin derived from the *Cinnamomum camphora* tree, native to the Koreas, China, Taiwan, Vietnam, and Japan. Camphor is known for its insect-repellent nature (it's the main scent throw to mothballs), and medicinally it aids as an insecticide, antifungal, antimicrobial, and antiviral and has antitussive (cough-suppressing) properties and constituents known to inhibit cancer. Spiritually, camphor supports strong purification work and repels low-vibrational entities and ghosts. It helps create strong psychic boundaries, and it is another strong Spirit evoked through spiritual fumigatory ceremonies. "Camphor, we call you here to work with us in our ceremony, guide our visions, and assist us in clearing our blockages and removing all things that may haunt us. Spirit of Camphor, aid our balanced growth and repair our immune systems so they may be fully alert and responsive. Camphor, be present in our work." Breathe three times and add to jar.

Note: Camphor is extremely harsh on the lungs. If you burn it on charcoals, please do so in a well-ventilated area, and if you fumigate an indoor space, leave the area for a couple of hours before returning, and open all windows when you do.

6. Guinea pepper/grains of paradise[5] (*Aframomum melegueta*), also known as melegueta pepper and alligator pepper, is a member of the ginger family, along with cardamom. Native to the tropical regions of West Africa, Guinea pepper is another culinary, medicinal, and magico-spiritual botanical. Medicinally, it warms digestion, treats diarrhea, supports cardiovascular health, stabilizes blood sugar, and is an anti-inflammatory. Spiritually, Guinea pepper gives energy to our ability to speak our desires into reality (especially when we haven't spoken truthfully or spoken our truth fully). It is also known to "heat up" romantic situations as well as aid in employment matters. "Guinea

---

5   As a Bruje I look at the relationships between plants within the same family to see how they speak individually and within their communities. Part of what I would like to offer my readers is not just a listing of ingredients and their properties but more a pedagogical line of inquiry within Brujería. Consider how ginger and Guinea pepper might be related both biologically and in their emanating Spirit. How do they address similar conditions but with their own personality?

Pepper, energize our tongues to speak into existence our deepest desires. Aid our efforts to manifest these visions, and show us how to use our energies to complete the tasks ahead. Spirit of Guinea Pepper, come forth and join us in this work." Breathe three times and add to jar.

7. Brugmansia/floripondio is also called angel's trumpet or yellow or white bell flower. *Brugmansia* is a genus of a number of bell-like flowering trees in the Solanaceae family. Related to datura and night-shade, brugmansia is one of the most toxic ornamental plants grown throughout South, Central, and North America and the Caribbean. Native to the Andes mountain ranges in Peru, Ecuador, Bolivia, and Chile, brugmansia species have properties engaged to treat asthma and cardiovascular imbalances, but their most recognizable aspects are hallucinogenic and euphoric in nature.

"Brugmansia, Spirit who helps us perceive the elevated unseen, invisible forces in our lives, help us to safely awaken our senses, and guide us with protection as we astrally take flight. Spirit of Brugmansia, be present in our work." Breathe three times and add to jar.

Note: Brugmansia should be handled with gloves and with great caution under the supervision of an expert. Even smelling the flower directly can be toxic. In this recipe it is engaged as a botanical spiritual essence.

Botanical Spiritual Essences

Instructions

★ Find the living plant or fresh plant material that you would like to create an essence from, making sure that it is healthy and thriving.

★ Ask permission of the plant or botanical to work with it; this can be as simple as energetically checking in and asking the plant to give you a physical sensation or sign that it is giving its consent to be worked with.

★ Make an offering (burn incense, sprinkle tobacco, give it some water, or leave three pennies) to its Spirit and thank it for being an ally, helper, and supporter.

★ Fill the bowl of water, place it in direct sunlight, and situate it under or around the plant.

★ This form of medicine is vibrational, and you want to be as emotionally balanced and present with this process as possible because the water will absorb your energies along with the botanical's. The entire process requires patience and takes three to four hours from start to finish.

In this first step there are two options for you to choose. Some Bruja(e)s gently dip the tip of a flower and allow it to drip into the bowl, while others absorb the energies by leaving the bowl in direct proximity to the botanical. The most important aspect here is to energetically hold space and call the plant's Spirit into the mixture. I suggest taking ninety minutes at minimum to infuse the spiritual essence of the plant into the water.

★ Now that you have created this medicine, the next step is to decant it. Using the funnel, fill the water halfway into the bottle and top off the remainder with a drop or two of a 100 proof alcohol (Everclear is great for both essences and tincture making). This mixture is called the "mother" and is a concentrated mixture that can be diluted and added into smaller bottles.

★ After you have closed and sealed the bottle, thank the plant for its medicine and essence. Now you can leave and return home. Once home, bottle it by filling 20 milliliter glass vials three-quarters full with purified or spring water then adding one full dropper of alcohol and one full dropper of the mother.

Dosage and Storage: Plant and flower essences are energetic in nature and don't have the same dosages as tinctures or other medicinals. They can be used more freely as well as added into teas, baths, perfumes, and incense recipes. To use internally, place a dropper full of essence under the tongue or into a glass of water. The effects of these essences kick in quickly and can last three to four hours, but mileage varies with each individual. Stored in a dark area away from heat sources, essences can last for two to three years.

---

8. Tobacco, or nicotiana (*Nicotiana* genus), is a member of the Solanaceae family, like brugmansia, and has several species. Currently grown as the main component of cigarettes and smoking blends, tobacco has been engaged as a ceremonial plant since humanity began populating the Americas. Medicinal uses include treatments for gout, respiratory distress, parasitic illnesses, and deep depressive episodes. In parts of the Amazon the link between tobacco and practicing medicine is so strong that the title of community physician means tobacco.

Spiritually, tobacco is a huge helper botanical due to its gifts of carrying humanity's prayers, intentions, and thoughts to the Creator. When working with tobacco, we need to be mindful of our thoughts because they will be communicated directly. Known as a protective and clearing medicine, tobacco assists in accessing the sacred both internally and in our environments and promotes good character and right relationships in all matters. "Spirit of Tobacco, help us to awaken to the voice of the Creator inside of us and the reflection of the Sacred no matter where we are. Spirit of honoring, wisdom, and ancestral knowledge, carry our prayers to the Source and assist us in staying in good character and right relationships no matter the situation. Tobacco, we ask that you work with us in this medicine." Breathe three times and add to jar.

Note: Tobacco is another botanical that must be worked with responsibly, especially if ingested.

9. Sage (*Salvia* genus) has many native varieties throughout the Americas besides white sage (*Salvia alpina*). Due to the current commodification of white sage, it is now considered an endangered species. Medicinally, all varieties of sage are helpers for issues such as sore throat, heartburn, and loss of appetite, and their chemical derivatives have shown benefits in treating memory loss, Alzheimer's, dementia, and depression. As a spiritual ally, sage is associated with clearing and purifying the self and spaces, connecting with Source and internal divinity, creating healthy boundaries, communicating truthfully and honestly, and being aware and conscious of ourselves and our footprints, both environmentally and in relationship with other people. "Spirit of Sage, we call you here to work with us in this medicine. Spirit of conscious awareness, help us to be aware of ourselves and how we are present internally and in spaces with one another. Help us to be right sized for every situation and to see our impacts in the world. Spirit of clarity, cleansing, and purification, help us to find our own clarity, to cleanse ourselves of all that is inhibiting our growth, and support our prioritization of healthy boundaries and connectedness to internal Source. Help us to claim our internal wholeness and identify thoughts, narratives, and internalized oppressions that voice anything to the contrary."

Scent Distinctions

1. Base Notes: Benzoin, sandalwood, and labdanum.

Benzoin resins and oils are derived from several trees of the *Styrax* genus, predominantly *Styrax benzoin* and *Styrax paralleoneurus*, native to Java, Sumatra, and Thailand. Medicinally, benzoin can protect minor wounds from inflammation and infection and assists in treating canker and bed sores, skin ulcers, and cracking skin conditions. Spiritually, benzoin clears through sweetening, raising the vibration of the area, and attracting positive beings into a space. Known for its healing and vitality-stimulating nature, benzoin has solar correspondences and can assist in meditation (inward illumination), mood elevation (rising out of the depths), and the warming of the heart (processing pent-up emotions and feelings of emotional numbness). "Spirit of Benzoin, warmer of the heart and sweetener of the ways, we call to you to be in this medicine to assist us in being sweeter, warmer, and gentler with ourselves and others. We ask that you clear away any low-vibrating, negative energy within us, our emotions, and our thoughts, as you clear it away from this space. Spirit of solar regeneration and vitality, awaken our inner vitality and help us to find kindness no matter the labor." Breathe three times and add to jar.

Labdanum (*Cistus ladanifer*), like benzoin, is found as both a resin and an oil and is extracted from cistus shrubs indigenous to eastern and western regions of the Mediterranean (southern Europe, Egypt, Turkey, and southwestern Asia). As a medicinal helper labdanum works with issues such as lung support and bronchitis, edema (water retention and swelling), and hardening of the spleen and as a stimulant and laxative.

Spiritually, labdanum acts like an energetic scab, sealing over the abrasion and healing the trauma from the inside. It also is deeply connected to transgenerational healing and can identify, mend, and repair ancestral hurts that are voiced in our bodies. "Spirit of Labdanum, with your gentle, sweet, and attentive nature, be present in our medicines. Help us to identify emotional and energetic wounds, and aid us in effectively treating and sealing the trauma. Healer who mends from the inside out, ally yourself in our healing journey. Help us to effectively repair past hurts and ensure that our energies are able to redouble in their vitality." Breathe three times and add to jar.

In combination, benzoin, sandalwood, and labdanum create an accord that mimics the smell of *Succinum* (amber harvested from conifers that include pine) and other semipetrified ambers engaged in incense-making and fumigatory recipes. Providing the base notes in this Florida Water recipe, this is the longest-lasting part of the fragrance throw and can mask the menthyl in the camphor and other bitter scents from the tincture base.

2. Heart Notes: Neroli, ylang-ylang, and jasmine.

Ylang-ylang (*Cananga odorata*) is the narcotically sweet flower of the cananga tree, which grows in Malaysia, the Philippines, Indonesia, and Thailand. Ylang-ylang is one the major ingredients in Agua Kananga spiritual water recipes. As a medicinal helper it works with gout, malaria, asthma, rheumatism, and digestion. In Traditional Chinese Medicine ylang-ylang is categorized as a cool and moist botanical correlating to the yin energy and is associated with the passions and life-giving principles of fire balanced with earth. Spiritually, it is an aphrodisiac promoting vulnerability and positive sexual attention by engaging traumas that can make people shy away from their sexual selves. Ylang-ylang unites desire, sensuality, passion, and emotionality, ensuring that our consciousness is aligned with our heart. "Spirit of Ylang-Ylang, we call you into our medicines to intoxicate our lives, hearts, minds, and spirits with the awe of creation. Spirit of Aphrodisia, awaken our senses to the love we have for ourselves and all those we care about. Assist with courage as we explore sensuality and pleasure." Breathe three times and add to jar.

Play with this heart note accord and see how you like it. Because Agua Florida is citrus forward, neroli is the star, with jasmine and ylang-ylang acting as support. As they are layered on top of the amber, they create a floral, citrus, honey fragrance.

3. Top Notes: Bergamot and pink peppercorn. Similar to the top notes in the Agua Florida above, we are bringing the pink peppercorn forward with the bergamot sparkle behind it. The floral spice, as it evaporates, gives way to the sweet citrus and then to the amber base.

Agua Florida Uses

Below are a number of different uses for Agua Florida and some instructions and ideas for how to employ it as spiritual medicine.

★ Clears and elevates spaces

★ Revives and stimulates physical energy

★ Sweetens and attracts high-vibrating forces

★ Cools anxiety, tensions, and chaotic thoughts

★ Aids in rewiring the fight-or-flight responses in the body

★ Invites peace and tranquility into our lives

★ Connects self with source

How to Use

★ **Self-cleansing:** Sprinkling a sizable amount in your palms and rubbing them together, guide your hands over the body, starting at the head and moving downward toward the bottoms of the feet while visualizing that you are washing away the energetic residues of the day.

★ **Cleaning spaces and altars:** Sprinkle or spray it in your spaces, just like smudging except with a liquid; remember to say your intent as you sprinkle and spray. You can also dampen a cleaning cloth with it and wipe over all surfaces. Agua Florida is a great way to clear any stagnant or low-lying energies on the altars, especially if you have been doing deep-cleaning, cleansing, or clearing work.

★ **Laundry wash:** When added to the last rinse cycle, Agua Florida washes any energetic residues away and leaves the clothes smelling fresh and new.

★ **To calm and revitalize:** Take a handkerchief and lightly soak it with Agua Florida, then put it in a zip-top bag and freeze it. This gives you a great rescue remedy to place over your eyes or forehead when you are feeling physically or spiritually fatigued. Remember that with all these uses, it's your intent that brings out the medicine; say it out loud!

★ **Honoring and carrying prayers:** When placed in a small container with water, this mixture can be prayed into and left on the altars to communicate your intents and desires.

★ **Tranquility and reconciliation spiritual work:** Use Agua Florida as a core ingredient for your recipes and spells. You will discover more of these recipes in the following chapters.

Chapter 3

LIMPIAS

The Art of Spiritual Cleansing

What happens when we feel stuck, aimless, and underwater, and how do we support ourselves and those we care about? Limpias (physical and spiritual cleansings) are more than just running an egg down our bodies or being swept ritually with herbs and potions. Those ceremonies are the outward performance of larger energetic and spiritual conversations happening between ourselves, our resources (herbs, potions, and incenses), our bodies, our spiritual courts, and the Creator. They are also not one-size-fits-all experiences where we can take a pill and be cured. Limpias are catalysts that open the door to health, balance, upliftment, and evolution, and more often than not they require ongoing sessions versus "one and we're done." On both ends, as the healer and the client, we are called into active participation (addressing the root cause of the issue instead of the symptom) in order to create long-lasting change and fundamentally shift any of these conditions.

Similar to Western clinicians, Curanderas (traditional medicine makers and healers) and Brujas go through long years of intense study, training, and mentoring before they are recognized as healers capable of doing the work. An important part of these trainings deals with not only identifying the root causes of illness and imbalance and effectively treating them, but also how we as healers clean ourselves after our work with clients so that we don't absorb those conditions. I have known many Curanderas who have died way too young of fast-spreading illness and disease, and in these traditions, it is partly attributed to the illnesses being transferred onto the healer instead of released by the client. It is not my intent to scare anyone away from doing limpias for themselves or their loved ones, but it requires much more study for us to be skillful enough to work for the public.

Psychic, Spiritual, and Emotional Ailments

Thought comes before action, and shifts in consciousness come before behavior modifications. In Brujería we work on the physical body in order to shift the emotional and spiritual bodies, knowing that as these etheric energies come into alignment, our physical selves will find their natural balances again. Below are some of the most well-known ailments and how they can affect our physical selves.

Susto or espanto: Fright, shock, "soul loss," or loss of the shadow. It can manifest as being easily startled, constant heart palpitations for unknown reasons, an inability to move on, high levels of anxiety, feeling "disembodied," fears that negative things will continue to happen again, a feeling that something is missing or of being lost and out of control, unexplained sadness, lack of appetite, loss of self-interest, uncontrollable bouts of crying, looking over one's shoulder and waiting for the other shoe to drop, nervousness, involuntary muscle tics, and extreme drowsiness during the day and insomnia at night. Susto is similar to post-traumatic stress disorder (PTSD)-related energetics and symptoms.

Mal ojo or envidia: Mal ojo (the evil eye) is the result of being targeted by envy and negative thoughts and intentions from others. Mal ojo is thought to heat up the blood, causing physical symptoms such as diarrhea, crying, vomiting, and a gassy stomach. It can have strong psychological effects as well, from shying away from attention or notice, to patterns of underachieving or not wanting praise or attention. There are usually signs of extreme and constant bullying, degrading treatment, and being intentionally targeted because of difference (being the lowest in the pecking order).

Bilis: Translated as "bile," bilis represents suppressed anger, aggression, and explosive tendencies. It can manifest as periods of extreme rage as well as dissociative elements in the personality. Bilis usually has ties to deep ancestral hurts that get replayed unconsciously through the generations. It has been my experience that perpetrators of domestic violence usually have some of these underlying tendencies and issues.

Mal aire and mal viento: Literally "bad air," mal aire signifies that a person has been exposed to physical and metaphysical "cold winds" and miasma. Spiritually it takes the form of environmental negativity that can overwhelm and weaken a person spiritually, mentally, physically, and psychically.

Pesar: Deep grief or heaviness on the heart and spirit that manifests from deep loss. Spiritually it can feel like something is feeding off of us and causing deep hopelessness and depression.

Embrujado: Bewitched or spiritually trapped or captured; an umbrella term for all types of negative workings people can do on each other.

Ways of diagnosing witchcraft usually involve deliberation and divination with an Elder you trust.

Mal prójimo: Translated as bad or evil neighbors, this form of ailment is caused by the negative thoughts and feelings of the people closest to us intentionally or unintentionally shooting poisons and toxins in our direction (poisoned arrows). Described by some as negative vibrations meant to cause destruction and harm to an individual.

Duende: An illness caused by an encounter with a spirit being (parasitic, energetic hitchhiker like a ghost or other entity) that one has picked up unknowingly. These presences can be tied to places like cemeteries, hospitals, and funeral parlors (anywhere that the dead reside) as well as low-vibrating environments that attract malicious beings, like prisons, derelict spaces that house unwell people, and sometimes even street corners where a number of accidents have occurred.

Shadow depletion: Our shadows are seen as our spiritual twins that were birthed at the same moment we were and the only beings that will be physically with us every second of our lives. While the shadow "lives in the astral or etheric worlds," it supports our vitality and desires to be physically incarnated. Shadow depletion happens when we get into states of continual depletion, trauma, deep illness, and stress.

How do we empower ourselves, and what tools do we have at our disposal?

NATURE CLEANSING/
OXYGEN CLEANSING

Most people forget that the natural world is right outside our doors. When I lived in Sonoma County, one of my favorite activities was to walk deep into the Armstrong Woods and let all the vegetation cleanse me (absorb all my stress, worry, anxiety) while breathing in the oxygenated air of the forest. I realize that not everyone lives near a nature preserve, but we have access to trees, grass, plants, and the earth and sky in most locations that I have traveled. I think it becomes a challenge for people to think that the trees and botanicals we see growing in our sidewalks or in city parks are "nature," but they are, and we can be in connection with them even more so than an isolated forest in the middle of nowhere. The following exercise will help in developing connections to the landscapes and nature that are always present in your life.

Find a tree, rock, patch of ground, or body of water, and chill. Fight the instincts that you have to do something, and just be still. Let yourself simply experience and be present in your body, mind, and Spirit. Try 10- to 20-minute sessions two to three times in a week, and journal about the experience. How does the landscape change throughout the seasons? What types of plants, animals, and mineral beings are present? (Don't forget that humans are also part of nature and should be taken into account as part of this exercise.) These are types of experiences that help develop allyship between you and the land you inhabit and open the paths to discovering what types of magics are already present in your surroundings. An old Brujería proverb states that both the illness and cure arise from the same environment and that the most poignant magics are usually found in your own backyard.

As a way of creating energetic reciprocity, consider taking a thanks-giving gift, like a couple of pennies, a splash of water, or a pinch of tobacco as an offering for the companionship. Just as you would never go to a get-together without a gift for the host, consider doing the same in the natural world. They are hosting and inviting you into connection, and offerings are a sign that you are willing to show generosity in return.

EVERGREEN DRY CLEANSING

No matter where I have been in the world—be it New York, San Francisco, Miami, Mexico City, Sicily, Malta, or Nigeria—I can find some sort of evergreen within a block of where I'm staying. If I have had an intense day, before I jump in the car or go home, I try to shake whatever energies that have been picked up both internally and on my physical body by performing this ritual. Remember that it's not about needing a "thing" to complete the work; it's about recognizing that all of nature is an ally, and you can use it to enhance the power that comes from within you, see chapter 4 (juniper), chapter 5 (fir), and chapter 6 (pine and cedar).

any evergreen
an offering

1. Find an evergreen that speaks to you, but please don't choose one that is dying or looks diseased—you want a healthy plant.

2. Take a moment to feel into the botanical and see if it wants to work with you. Usually if a plant is in agreement, the energies are settled and relaxed, but if it's a "no," you most definitely will feel it in your senses. You will learn to trust your instincts and what you are phys-ically, mentally, emotionally, and spiritually feeling and sensing. You are inviting the Spirits internally versus expecting them to externally appear before you.

3. Give the offering to the plant and thank it. (It doesn't have to be an oratory; a simple "Thank you for working with me" is great.)

4. Gently break off a small to medium-sized handful of the herb.

5. Take in its presence and take a deep breath of its aroma (really smell it and let that sensory experience sink in).

6. Now you are going to verbally pray and speak your petition for the botanical to wash you clean of any negative experiences, energies, forces, entities, or situations that are on you and release them from your body, mind, heart, and Spirit.

7. Starting at the crown, move in circular, sweeping motions (clockwise and counterclockwise), around the top of your head; the forehead and the sides and back of your head; then to your third eye; ears; the complete back of your head; your entire face, concentrating on the eyes, nose, and mouth; down the chin and the full front and back of the neck; across both shoulders; the back of the shoulders and lower neck, down the front and back of the arms, armpits, and hands; then down the chest, concentrating on the heart, lungs, ribcage, sides of the torso, stomach, belly button, and front of the genitals; then as much of the back as you can reach—kidneys, back of the intestines, lungs, and heart. Now move to the front and back of your hips; perineum; then the buttocks—both cheeks; down the front and backs of the thighs, front and back of the knees; front and back of the shins, front and back of the ankles, and finally, the top, bottom, and sides of your feet. By the end you should be feeling really good and a bit lighter in your energy. (When I get home I usually spray myself down with something or take a spiritual bath to further release any toxins.)

8. After the physical cleansing I usually clap three times, make a noise, or stomp my feet to energetically shift from the spiritual work to everyday consciousness as well as to indicate to Spirit that the ritual itself is over.

9. Say one final thank you to the living botanical and then take the remains of your cleansing bundle and dispose of them in a place of nature (or if they are really gunky and full of your spiritual poo, you can put them in the trash). Once disposal has happened, don't look back or return to that area for the rest of the night.

SPIRITUALLY CLEANING THE SELF AND OTHERS WITH SACRED SMOKES

For a more detailed description of a sacred smoke cleansing, as well as a full list of types of smoke blends, prayers, and instructions on how to work with incense charcoal and burners, see https://ulyssespress .com/books/the-modern-art-of-brujeria for a link to additional content.

1. Begin with verbal prayer and ask the resins and herbs to work with you and the Creator to purify and cleanse, help to release all negativity and obstacles, and restore harmony and balance within yourself and others.

2. Start at the front of the face and gently waft the smoke toward the face and over your head (making sure you aren't holding your breath because you want to breathe a little of the smoke). Waft the smoke in the directions of the eyes, third eye, ears, nose, and mouth, and then usher the smoke up over the crown and to the back of the head.

3. Now move down to front and back of the neck, across the shoulders and tops of the arms. Then move to the bottoms of the arms and to the back of the shoulder blades. Next, the top and bottoms of the hands.

4. Next, move to the front, back, and sides of the torso, concentrating on the heart, lungs, solar plexus, stomach, intestines, and kidneys.

5. Then to the front, back, and sides of the genitals and hips. Next, under the perineum with your smokes. (If you are working on other people, be respectful, ask permission, and you can even waft the smoke in that direction—my intention is to avoid further traumatizing someone who comes to me for help.) Now buttocks, making sure to address both cheeks.

6. Finally, move to the front and back of the thighs, knees, shins, ankles, and tops and bottoms of the feet.

7. Remember that throughout this process you are calling on the Spirits of the herbs and the Creator to do the work versus your own Spirit doing the heavy lifting. I have seen people completely exhaust themselves after cleansing a single individual because they were using their personal energy instead of stepping back and letting the botanicals and the big folks (divinities, guides, and helpers) handle the business.

8. Take a moment to fully gather yourself and thank all the Beings who advocated for you (and the client) during the process, and at this stage the ritual is complete.

Note: Sometimes I feel led to concentrate on different parts of the body or ring bells or rattles as part of this process. There are many varieties and ways of working with sacred smokes, but the most important aspect is to let Spirit guide you. Remember that these recipes and steps are guides pointing the way for all of us to understand how our own Spirits speak versus a pass-or-fail mentality.

SPIRITUALLY CLEANING AND PROTECTING A SPACE

Sacred Resins Incense (page 175)

Uncrossing Bath (chapter 4)

Double Action Reversing Candle (chapter 7)

Love and Good Fortune Wash (chapter 4)

olive oil or any protection oil (chapters 6 and 7)

1. Clean the space physically and get rid of all clutter and trash.

2. Follow the same procedure each time, employing the Sacred Resins Incense blend first, then the Uncrossing Bath, and finally the Double Action Reversing Candle.

★ **Open all doors, cabinets,** and storage areas because you want the smokes, bath, and flame to disperse throughout every corner of your living space so that the Spirit of your botanicals and the Creator can touch all the surfaces.

★ **Starting at the entranceway,** begin with the incense blend, let it smolder, and then guide the smoke from top to bottom and back to front. Next, you will create three equilateral crosses. This represents the four directions and elements in harmony throughout the physical, emotional/mental, and spiritual realms. While guiding the smoke, verbally speak your intent and invite the botanical into the space. "Spirit of these Sacred Resins, essences of purification, clarity, and insight, you are welcomed into this space. I call you forth with this sacred smoke to cleanse all obstacles, stagnation, and negating forces from this space and ensure that they do not return. From all corners and all directions, I purify and cleanse this space in the Creator's name."

★ **Walking to the farthest room of the area,** methodically repeat these same actions while physically voicing your intents, covering every threshold, wall, corner, window, closet, and cabinet with the sacred smokes. If there are multiple levels to the area you are cleansing, start from the top and move to the bottom and work from the back to the front.

★ **Now that you have made a complete circuit,** moving from the entrance to the area farthest away and coming full circle, repeat the gestures one final time while saying, "Spirit of our Sacred Smokes, thank you for your work and support, I ask that you continue to cleanse and guard this space. Let only positive and uplifting energies, forces, and people enter here."

★ **Using this procedure as an example,** follow up this fumigation process with the Uncrossing Bath mixture and flame. Here are two examples of prayers that can be engaged for both bath and flame: "Uncrossing Wash, Spirit that cuts, clears, and cleanses all forms of negativity, illness, unbalanced energies, and uninvited spirits, I call to you to remove these forces from myself and this space immediately; wash, clean, and rebalance this area and let only positivity, blessings, and peace remain here. Restore, rejuvenate, and replenish this area with your grace." "Reversing Candle, Spirit that burns through and returns all evil, negativity, obstacles, blockages, and uninvited spirits, clean, clear, and rebalance this area immediately! Assist me as I fully claim these spaces both inside and out, and protect me and this area from energetic trespassers and those who consciously or unconsciously do not have my best interests at heart. Spirit of Reversing, undo all evil and return it back to sender."

3. Now you will move on to the blessing work, which protects the space and fills it with all the positive and blessed forces of Creation. Remember that when you do cleansing work, a vacuum is created in the energies, and in order for them not to be filled immediately with negatively, you employ blessing and fortune work to ensure that those spirits and forces can't come back in. In this instance you will be utilizing the Boundary Setting and Protection Incense Blend and the Love and Good Fortune Wash (it's a bath when employed on the body and a wash when engaged for spaces).

★ **Moving in reverse order this time,** you will be going from bottom to top, front to back—literally inviting the blessings into every corner of the house starting at the threshold. Your first step begins again with the doorway, but this time you will be gesturing as mentioned above—bottom to top, front to back—creating three crosses in the air. While you are gesturing and guiding the smoke, speak aloud the intentions:

★ **"Spirit of this protection blend,** help me to connect with my highest self and awaken my Holy Guardians and Protectors both within me and within my spaces. I ask that you walk with me and create the path for blessings and the Creator to enter my life and my space. Be a sentinel of protection in my home and let only joy, laughter, and love enter here."

★ **Following the cleansing steps in reverse order,** you will make your way throughout the area, hitting all the corners, shelves, nooks, and crevices. (Remember, work from bottom to top, front to back, until you return to the threshold.) Now that you have made this last circle of the area with the sacred smoke, complete the gestures one last time and thank the Spirit of Frankincense. "Spirit of this Protective Sacred Smoke, I thank you for your support and assistance; continue to be present within me and within this space."

★ **Now follow the same methods and procedures with the Love and Good Fortune Wash.** "Good Fortune and Love, I call to you to bless and support this space with abundant blessings, riches, loving emotions, thoughts, actions, and energies and to raise the vibrations, hearts, and Spirits of all those who enter here. Be with me, Fortune and Love, be my ally, supporter, and guide and ensure that wherever I am in the world, your presence is always close."

★ **Finally,** seal the threshold, front and back doors, and windows with olive oil or a protection blend of your choosing. You seal these areas with a five-point pattern (four corners and the center) and verbally speak aloud your intentions and prayers surrounding both the blessings you want to invite and how you want them to enter your life; and furthermore, that these thresholds are sealed and protected against all negating energies and forces. "Protection Oil, help me to guard and protect this space from all unwanted, uninvited, and negative beings, spirits, forces, and people. Be my safeguard and guardian, and only those with good intents and positive energies can enter."

Chapter 4

BAÑOS Y LAVADOS ESPIRITUALES

The Art of Spiritual Baths and Washes

Water as a conduit for spiritual, magical, and religious practices arises globally across cultures and time. Water refreshes, cools, clears, cleans, moves electrical currents, holds memory, sustains life, and helps organisms flourish—all of these concepts and forms are present in Brujería.

Physical and spiritual hygiene are less about "cleanliness" and more about the processes we engage in for cultivating health. Taking a shower, sweeping the floors, and brushing our teeth are not just ways of removing dirt and grime but are about creating the optimal conditions for thriving. Just as we clean our homes and our bodies, spiritual hygiene is necessary to shed, clear, strengthen, and beautify ourselves from the inside out. By performing rituals as we bathe physically, we can also cleanse ourselves spiritually, fostering the outcomes we want to see in our lives. In this chapter, we will discover the different ways we can engage washes and baths to build your Brujería tool kit.

Baños

Baños, or baths, come in a variety of mediums and formulations. As an introduction to this work, I have included a short list of some of the more common types that you will find at most botanicas (Brujería shops) as well as metaphysical stores.

★ **Despojos:** The word *despojo* translates as "dispossession," and despojos strip and cut ties between the self and unwanted connections and forces, flush out obstructions and obstacles, rip and tear away layers of residual psychic and energetic detritus, and are useful for dealing with spirit possessions (places where we aren't fully in control and another consciousness is working out unresolved issues).

★ **Bitter and Breaking:** Similar to despojos, bitter and breaking baths break stagnant conditions, releasing spiritual heat, uncrossing our paths and clearing our confusions, releasing unresolved emotional disturbances and things that we have picked up from others or the environment. Bitter baths help with the detoxification and digestion processes on a spiritual level, and some of the herbs also stimulate and support liver, gallbladder, and intestinal health and maintenance.

★ **Sweetening and Attracting:** Just as the name implies, sweetening and attracting baths are intended to uplift our vibrations, attract blessings, and support our health, and they are underutilized in protection *trabajos* (spiritual workings and rituals). The vast majority of practitioners think that protection only involves fighting things off or aggressively guarding your space. Overall, these baths are meant to bring joy and hope back into our lives and our homes while creating the conditions for us to fully meet and hold onto our blessings.

★ **Strengthening, Securing, and Protecting:** Similar to sweet baths, strengthening, securing, and protecting bath workings help to build ourselves up, secure our boundaries and properties, and guard against unwanted and uninvited people, forces, and energies.

★ **Controlling and Dominating:** These baths support us having the upper hand in all dealings and having others acquiesce to our thoughts, visions, energies, and ideas.

Lavados

Just like baths, lavados, or washes, engage similar conditions and are distinguished mainly by their employment. Created to work with physical spaces, to bathe and charge items, and to wash specific areas of the body, lavados usually have higher concentrations of alcohol- and oil-based formulas than baths.

★ **Floor:** Used to both clear and cleanse our physical spaces as well as to protect and bless.

★ **Business:** Used to clear poverty, bad luck, and negative energies from our lives while attracting consistent customers.

★ **Laundry:** Can be used on our laundry to further carry the energies in our lives. As people come across us, they pick up and carry the spell on them.

★ **Body:** Specific parts of our bodies can be washed to attract certain energies—hands for gambling and money, head for perception and clarity, feet for stamina and strength, the genitals for attraction and love.

Timing, Phases, and Working with the Seasons

When we perform our workings can be of consideration as different times of the day and year generate different energies. These are some general ideas and ways of thinking about timing our baños and lavados, but the number one rule of Brujería is to do things when we need them and not to wait until it's the "right time." Timing is meant to add to our workings (as opposed to the idea that if you don't do them at a specific day or time they will fail). In the list below I outline days and times throughout the week matched with their spiritual associations.

Times of Day

★ **Midnight, 3 a.m., sunrise:** Uncrossing/breaking/cleansing/clearing, astral work, blessings from the elders of the night and the unseen forces

★ **6 a.m.–9 a.m.:** Ancestral work

★ **9 a.m.–noon:** Blessing and attraction workings

★ **Noon–6 p.m.:** Protection, shielding, strengthening, building

★ **6 p.m.–9 p.m.:** Blessings and attraction workings

★ **9 p.m.–midnight:** Ancestral workings

★ **11:30 p.m.–12:30 a.m.:** Negative hour (in Brujería and Conjure traditions of the Southern United States, 11:30–12:30 is seen as an in-between time when energetic portals open for maleficent entities)

★ **Midnight–3 a.m.:** Negative hours in which the unrestful dead are especially active

★ **3 a.m.–6 a.m.:** Blessings of the Creator, dreaming true, visionary experiences, and prophecy hours, astral travel, and revitalization of life

Days of the Week

★ **Sunday:** Uncrossings and cleansings, ancestral work, peace, tranquility, meditation, home and family life, healing, vitality

★ **Monday:** Road opening, communication, money drawing, protection, security, intuition and perception building, beautification

★ **Tuesday:** Clearing, strengthening, protecting, courage, passion, desire, goal-oriented magics

★ **Wednesday:** Writing, studying, success, victory, inspiration, public or community-driven matters

★ **Thursday:** Business, politics, legal matters, divination, leadership, strategizing, breaking addictions

★ **Friday:** Love, money, friendships, connectivity, partnerships, artistry, fun, partying

★ **Saturday:** Protection, manifestation, completion, family and home, starting things off with discipline

Lunar

★ **New Moon:** Cleansing, uncrossing, fresh starts

★ **Waxing Moon:** Gradually increases blessings, luck, fortunes, love

★ **Full Moon:** Height of the blessings, experiencing the fullness of the manifestation

★ **Waning Moon:** Takes things away, banishes, moves things out and away

- ★ **First day of each lunar period:** Represents the beginning of that lunar phase's energies and is the traditional day that we would start the baths

Seasons

- ★ **Fall:** Harvesting our goals, manifesting long projects, seeing the fruition of our labors

- ★ **Winter:** Resting, visioning, building ourselves up, replenishing

- ★ **Spring:** Planting, sprouting, hatching, creating new projects

- ★ **Summer:** Growing, thriving, cultivating, enjoying, experiencing

- ★ **New Year:** Starting off the year fresh! In many countries in the Americas with coastal regions, there is a traditional midnight bath taken at the ocean. To practice this, strip down nude and swim out a distance from shore. At midnight, facing the beach, use the first seven waves to propel you forward while verbally speaking a manifestation goal for the New Year.

WORKING WITH USED SPIRITUAL BATHWATER—DISPOSALS

In many of the traditions of Brujería instructions are given for the disposal of used bathwater, but most of the time no one explains why. The used bathwater represents the totality of the ritual (the water holds the magic and remembers the petition), and by disposing of it in certain ways, the practitioner creates an energetic pathway or river that manifests the intent of the work. Below are times and locations for disposing of used bathwater and their intended uses.

★ **Sunrise:** Open possibilities, step into the new day.

★ **Sunset:** To remove a negative situation, influence, force, or person, to have them leave like the sun is leaving the sky.

★ **Crossroads:** Purification, block buster, remove witchcraft, move out of what our current experience is into something completely new.

★ **In the wilds or place of nature:** Similar to crossroads—to take things away from us and not have them follow us back home; to move beyond what we are living and create a new pathway.

★ **Trees:** Asking the tree to take the energies (usually uncrossing/breaking) from us and transform them. The tree acts both as an access point helping us to connect to the Creator and as an energetic substitute for us (the tree consents to taking on the illness or negativity itself).

★ **Large rocks and boulders:** To break long-standing, stagnant energies, when you feel like you are up against insurmountable odds.

★ **Streets:** Throwing used bathwater into the street scatters the energies as cars drive over it.

★ **Backyard:** To keep energies like love and money at home.

★ **Tracks:** Baths can be thrown into foot tracks for many reasons because these tracks are seen as a personal concern (an item linked to the individual, such as hair, writing samples, or clothes) that can be ritually worked to cause a reaction within the person whose tracks are used.

UNCROSSING BATH RITE (HOODOO TRADITION)

spiritual bath (recipes for spiritual baths start on page 83)

2 candles (tea lights work great)
clean clothes

Some important things to bear in mind about spiritual baths:

★ Historically, spiritual baths were taken in very particular ways. Feel free to luxuriate and soak in your bath; however, to work this rite you should also follow the traditional instructions following your soak.

★ You have two options for when to take your bath: dawn or midnight. Dawn means first light.

In determining what time to begin your bath, you will want to take into account whether or not you want to soak before moving into the rite itself. The time spent luxuriating or soaking in the bath should be used to focus on your intentions. If you incorporate this into your bath rite plan, you may want to begin 45 minutes before midnight or sunrise. Depending on my mood as well as if I have access to a tub, I might feel like going directly into the ritual versus having a soak. In those instances my timing is a bit freer and I start within 30 minutes of those times. Taking a midnight or sunrise bath means that you want to be at the crossroads at that time.

★ Spiritual baths are not "soap and lather" baths; rather, they are ritual baths. If you need to be "clean," take a bath or shower before you begin the work.

★ While taking your spiritual bath, the only light in the bathroom will be provided by the candles. Tea lights work great for this purpose, but ideally you want the candles to be white (if you follow color symbolism, you can also choose candles in colors that correspond to your intentions for your bath). You will place the candles on the floor, by the bathtub or shower, spacing them several feet apart. The idea is that the candles represent a doorway or threshold that you will enter or cross as you step into your bathtub or shower.

★ Don't blow out your candles after the bath. If you must extinguish them, snuff them out using a candle snuffer or your index finger and thumb. Ideally, you will want these candles to burn to completion (and this is one of the reasons the tea lights are so handy). I suggest before disposing of your bathwater at the crossroads (more information about this will follow) that you place your candles on an appropriate personal altar or in another special place.

★ After you have completed your bath rite, you should not towel dry but air dry.

★ Your bath may have herbs or residue of herbs in it, and these may stick to your skin as a result. Allow them to dry on your skin as you air dry. The point of air drying is to anchor the work you have done—you want to keep it on you.

★ When you have dried, you should put on clean clothes.

★ There may be herbal residue in your bathtub; the remnants can be wiped away later and do not require special disposal.

★ After you complete your bath, you may want to take time to observe your internal landscape. Observation and record keeping help to anchor the work you are doing, and you are encouraged to anchor your experience in ways that call you into presence. By so doing, you will cocreate (with the rite itself) the conditions you wish to cultivate.

★ Following your bath, pay attention to signs—those divinatory moments when you sense the mystery is conversing with you—during your waking life and your dream life.

★ Sometimes spiritual baths, as part of the work, bring up difficult issues. This is not always comfortable but can be a part of a process of release and transformation. It is important to support yourself to the best of your capabilities with the tools available to you when undergoing any spiritual work.

★ Though many people have noticeable shifts as a result of spiritual baths, everyone maintains a different chemistry with different rituals. After your spiritual bath you may not feel "fixed," but you will have deepened your engagement with those paradigms you wish to transform.

Instructions for taking a spiritual bath:

1. Pour your bath into a tub of hot water (or bucket or pail, if using a shower).

2. After you have your two candles lit, you will step through the space between them, as if they are a doorway, and thus step into your bath. Before you step into your bath, it is recommended that you do one of the following: make a prayer, state your intentions clearly, or recite an appropriate Psalm (the 23rd Psalm is a standard for such work).

3. After soaking and focusing on your intent, you will want to move into the rite itself. Using your pouring vessel, you will pour water from your head or neck down seven times. If you wish to preserve your hairdo, pour from the neck down. I highly recommend pouring from your head down. You will pour your water and enact the rite in the following manner (note: you will repeat this set of movements seven times in a row):

4. From the head or neck down, you will pour the water down the front of your body.

5. Each time before you pour the water, you will think of the conditions you want to remove and the aspects you want to cultivate. For some people this takes the form of a prayer, while for others it is enough to just allow the words to form. Either way, say it out loud!

6. You will do this series of gestures seven times in a row, and you may say the same prayer each time, or you may say a different prayer each time. It's up to you.

7. After you have said your prayer and poured the water down the front of your body, put your pouring vessel down. Now you will make these specific gestures:

8. Cross your arms like so: right hand on left shoulder and left hand on right shoulder.

9. Now you will brush down and across your body with both of your hands at the same time, uncrossing your hands as they come across your thighs. As you uncross your hands, say out loud, "Remove the condition from me."

10. Conclude by brushing down your thighs legs, and feet.

To recap, this will be the pattern, seven times in a row:

Prayer / pour water down your body / put down the pouring vessel / cross your arms over your chest / uncross your arms / conclude by brushing down your legs and feet.

★ When you have completed the rite and have air dried and put on clean clothes, you will dispose of your bathwater. In the olden days, people bathed in portable tubs outdoors, and to dispose of their bathwater they would simply tip the tub in an eastern direction. But most of us no longer bathe in this way. Instead, you will fill your pouring vessel with bathwater, and this will represent all of your bathwater. After you have your bathwater sample, the rest of the water can be let down the tub drain.

★ You will dispose of your bathwater by going to the crossroads. A crossroads is any place where two roads or paths cross. Once there, you will throw or pour your water toward the east, the direction of the rising sun.

★ It is typical to make a recitation after you dispose of your bathwater, in the form of a prayer or other improvised words. A simple "Amen" or "it is done" also works fine.

★ After you have released your water at the crossroads, turn around and walk home without looking back. Once home, you may want to sit in meditation or reflection.

SWEETENING BATH RITE

Sweetening baths are meant to be luxuriant and are very similar to uncrossing or breaking baths with some key differences:

1. Take your time to absorb the juiciness of this process because these baths help you magnify and radiate your intentions in the world.

2. Sweetening baths can generally be taken all hours of the day, and the timing is based on the conditions you are going through (for example, I would do a love bath before a date or a steady work bath before a job interview).

3. Instead of moving down the body, you will be stroking up from your feet to your head while praying for your goals and desires.

4. Similar to the Uncrossing Bath above on page 89, the water is collected for disposal, but instead of taking it to a crossroads, you can employ it in a number of different ways. Used love bathwaters can be sprinkled from the front door coming into the house and sprinkled on the path you would like the object of your love to follow (couch, kitchen, bed, and so on). Money baths can be sprinkled where you would like to attract clients and sprinkled to your front door, or they can be sprinkled where you keep your money and on your hands when you gamble.

SAMPLE BUSINESS WASH CEREMONY

Floor washes and general money magics became associated with Fridays due to weekly salaries being paid after work on Friday afternoons and evenings. These traditions have stayed constant even today, and part of my current practices revolves around road opening, block busting, and money workings to start attracting these blessings for the upcoming week.

1. The first step is prep work: physically and spiritually cleanse, purify, and seal your space.

2. Next, make the bath. Choose a formula appropriate to your needs, and I would suggest timing it with the New Moon cycle in order to grow your business, just like the moon will grow in the sky. Also consider timing it to the start of your business day or right before your busiest customer hours.

3. Fix two tea lights with a general money-drawing formula and place them at the threshold of the front door of the business.

4. Starting from the sidewalk or front entrance of the building, you will be scrubbing or sprinkling the floors with the money-drawing business wash, creating the path you want the customers to take to get to the cash register. While scrubbing and sprinkling, verbally say your intents and prayers and visualize leading the customers throughout the store, showing them where to spend their money and finally ending with the point of sale. Physically describe the experience you want them to have and the types of goods and services you would like them to buy.

5. Following with the sacred smoke mixtures aligned with your desires, start again at the sidewalk and walk the customers and the energy of money throughout the business and to the cash register while verbally speaking your intents and prayers.

6. Finally, fix and load a seven-day, glass-encased candle with the money-drawing formulas and walk it throughout the store one last time while again verbally speaking the intentions. Set this candle next to the cash register or on the money altar to complete the rite.

What to Expect Afterward

After you have completed the bath work, take time to observe your internal landscapes. It is extremely important to observe and journal to help to anchor the work as a way of bringing all of your senses of knowing to the table. By so doing, you cocreate (with the rite itself) the conditions to manifest these magics.

Following the bath, pay attention to signs—those divinatory moments when you sense the mystery is conversing with you—during your waking and dreaming lives.

Sometimes spiritual baths, as part of the work, bring up difficult issues. This is not always comfortable, but it can be a part of a process of release and transformation. Though many people experience noticeable shifts as a result of spiritual baths, everyone maintains a different chemistry with different rituals. After the spiritual bath you may not feel "fixed," but you will have deepened your engagement and magics, building toward your ultimate goals.

Now that you know how to use washes and take baths, let's move on to recipes that have been tried and tested in my own practice. For each recipe, start with a pitcher of water obtained from the source of your choice, gather your ingredients, and bless each one individually, exhaling on them three times before adding them to your pitcher.

Grocery Store Cleansing Bath

1 part rock salt

2 parts Epsom salt

3 parts sea salt

citrus (page 38)

rosemary (page 97)

yerba buena/mint (page 32)

thyme

chamomile

Salts: A natural cleanser, salt absorbs the physical and spiritual characteristics of anything that it touches. Rock salts cleanse and strengthen tissues and assist with cellular regeneration, Epsom salts have analgesic properties that release swelling and help with sore muscles, and sea salts carry the energies and Spirits of the oceans and seas and represent the unseen waves of expansive and benevolent assistance. "Spirit of Salts, help us to remember ourselves, and assist us in returning back to our natural states of Grace. Spirit that absorbs and cleanses, cleanse all negating forces and experiences that have caused pain, that have made us sore, and wash them away from us. Spirit of Salts, Spirit of Holiness and Spirit of Preservation, assist us as we persevere and replenish us for our journeys."

Citrus: Any citruses from the Agua Florida recipe can be used here, and I like to find the ones that are in season for my area.

Rosemary (*Salvia rosmarinus*): Rosemary, native to the Mediterranean and southwestern Asia, is medicinally known as a circulatory aid, memory booster, analgesic, and immune supporter. This helper is known spiritually to aid with peace, clarity, insight, and purification. "Spirit of Rosemary, stand with me in this work today. Spirit of peace, clarity, and tranquility, support me as I root myself in these energies. Guide my thoughts, emotions, and heart as I release all things that are troubling me, Spirit of Rosemary, be my guardian and protector.

Yerba buena/mint: See page 32.

Thyme (*Thymus vulgaris*): Indigenous to the Mediterranean region, thyme is an herb that has been utilized since antiquity. Thyme is a natural antiviral and antibiotic that is part of several medicinal recipes for treating bronchitis, whooping cough, sore throat, colic, arthritis, upset stomach, stomach pain (gastritis), and diarrhea. Spiritually, thyme is called on to reclaim health, especially after psychic attacks, assists in developing and deepening intuition and psychic receptivity, and attracts prosperity and money. In Southern traditions in the United States, thyme has the added benefit of giving us more "time" in terms of spellwork. "Thyme, come forward and help us in this work. Spirit that fights parasites and pathogens, help us to fight all energetic and psychic vampires and parasites in our lives. Help us to identify immediately who these people and forces are, remove them from our lives, and assist us as we reclaim ourselves fully in our power."

Chamomile (*Matricaria recutita*): Another well-known helper is manzanilla or chamomile flower, which is native to Europe, Africa, and Asia and is now a popular botanical in the Americas. Engaged as a supportive aid for digestive help, chamomile is also called on for its cooling, calming, and sedative qualities, as well as for its beauty aspect when added to skin and hair recipes. Spiritually, chamomile sweetens the roads and paths by tearing through obstacles and stagnant energies. "Spirit of Chamomile, essence of sweetness, beauty, and tranquility, help me as I court sweet blessings in my life. Assist me to clear away all bitter, harsh, and heating energies, and call forth tranquility and grace both inwardly and throughout my world. Walk with me in my life, Chamomile, and be my ally."

Traditional 13 Herb Crossroads Bath and Ritual

This is a *despojo*, or a bath that tears away circumstances, energies, entities, and long-standing negativity.

ocean water	agrimony
spring water	eucalyptus
hyssop	pine (page 100)

rue (page 58)

nettle

white clover flower

lemon (page 38)

yerba buena/mint (page 32)

rosemary (page 97)

juniper

fennel (page 57)

basil (page 30)

Ocean water: Represents the life-generating principles of the ocean and the resources it gives the world, specifically being fed by the ocean—the vastness, riches, and energy that is part of the natural world.

Spring or river waters: Represents movement, going with the flow, unblocking and uncrossing, attraction, pleasure, joy, sweetness.

Hyssop (*Hyssopus officinalis*): This is another botanical in the mint family, making it similar to its energetic cousins, and its native range extends from the Middle East to North Africa and the southern Mediterranean regions. Medicinally, hyssop is considered a stimulant, carminative (herb that relieves gas), and expectorant and is employed in treating colds, coughs, congestion, and lung complaints. Hyssop is shown to have calming and soothing qualities that can assist with nervous system imbalances and toothaches. Spiritually, hyssop is associated with purification rites by helping us to shed all layers of negativity and negative actions and reclaiming our wholeness and purity (we have lifted out everything that is not of us). "Spirit of Hyssop, be present in our work and help us to shed all negativity, negative self-reflections, and negative actions we have committed, and assist us in taking full accountability for our behaviors. Lift and elevate us, and in so doing help us to lift out everything that is not of our best interest and blessings. Spirit of Hyssop, be our guide and advocate for us continually."

Agrimony (*Agrimonia eupatoria* or *gryposepala*): There are 15 species of agrimony known throughout the world, with their native habitats ranging from Africa to the Northern Hemisphere. Common European agrimony is most often referenced in these types of workings, but I love the Central and North American variety because it has a bit more kick to it. Medicinally, agrimony was sometimes brewed into a tea and used as gargle for sore throats, while it was utilized externally as a mild antiseptic and astringent. Metaphysically associated with reversing any and all negativity and returning back to sender, agrimony is a powerful guardian, protector, and advocate for our well-being. "Spirit of Agrimony, we call to you today to help us cleanse and reverse all negativity and negative forces in our lives. Great guardian and protector, be with us as we affirm our boundaries and strengthen our fortitude."

Eucalyptus: Native to Australia and Tasmania, eucalyptus has a wide variety of species in its genus. Medicinally employed in respiratory steams as a decongestant, it has been engaged to treat ailments like sore throats, sinusitis, and bronchitis. In metaphysics, this botanical has similar associative properties in that it helps us to "cough up" any and all deep-seated negativity that might be constraining our abilities to spiritually breathe. "Spirit of Eucalyptus, assist us in expelling all low-level energies and negativity, and aid us we claim blessings, joy, and health in our lives. Spirit that expectorates any hidden or secret poisons, pathogens, and parasites, immediately remove these entities from ourselves and our lives."

Pine: A variety of trees in the *Pinus* genus and Pinaceae family, pines are indigenous to most of the Northern Hemisphere and some tropical regions of the Southern Hemisphere. Medicinally, pine aids the respiratory system, reducing inflammatory responses in the lungs;

supports blood pressure and cardiovascular health; and is engaged to treat colds, flus, and infections. Spiritually, pine is associated with peace, spiritual ascension, longevity and the eternal power of our Spirits, protection, refuge, and nourishing our lives. "Spirit of Pine, assist us today in nourishing our hearts, minds, and Spirits with your medicine. Spirit of peace and protection, support our elevation and walk with us throughout our lives."

Rue: See page 58.

Nettle (*Urtica dioica*): Indigenous to western North Africa and Eurasia, nettle has spread worldwide. Medicinally employed to treat joint and muscle pain, arthritis, gout, anemia, urinary tract infections, eczema, and anemia, nettle is also highly nutritional and has antioxidant components. Ritually, nettle is associated with breaking long-standing negative conditions, removing curses, exorcising unwanted and uninvited spirits, healing, protection, and, in certain formulas, inducing lust. "Spirit of Nettle with your stinging needles, protect us from all forces and entities that wish to cause us harm. Spirit of Purification, greater fighter that breaks all negative conditions, forces, and intentions, aid us in removing all jinxes and curses, and help us to exorcise all uninvited and unwanted spirits, forces, and entities. Be with us in our work, Holy Guardian Nettle."

White clover flower (*Trifolium repens*): Native to central Asia and Europe, white clover is medicinally known for its utilization in treating fever, coughs, and colds. Metaphysically, clover is linked to breaking stagnation and long-held bad luck, destroying jinxes, expelling evil, and attracting good luck. "Spirit of White Clover, assist us in removing outside interference, breaking stagnation, and uncrossing ourselves from jinxes, curses, and bad luck. Help us to identify all these conditions both inside and out and remove them from our lives, homes, and paths. Spirit of White Clover Flower, be present in our lives and be with us."

Lemon: See page 38.

Yerba buena/mint: See page 32.

Rosemary: See page 97.

Juniper: Juniper (*Juniperus*) is a genus of trees in the cypress family (*Cupressaceae*) and is found throughout the world, from the Arctic to Central America, from subtropical regions in Africa to Tibet. Medicinally associated with sugar regulation within the body and with lung and asthma support, it is a diuretic and antiseptic and has anti-arthritis properties. Juniper is another botanical with cross-cultural meanings, histories, and properties. Metaphysically associated with cleansing, blessings, protecting, and creating visionary experiences, Juniper is engaged in a variety of ways and methods. "Spirit of Juniper, I ask for your assistance in creating strong boundaries between myself and the Spirit Worlds. Assist me in communicating effectively, and protect me against any forces that try to possess or overcome me in any manner. Support me as I learn how to master my gifts and empower within me the strength and fortitude necessary to complete the work. Juniper, be with me."

Fennel: See page 57.

Basil: See page 30.

Love and Good Fortune Bath or Wash

This recipe is an excellent example of a sweetening bath that attracts positive influences, fortunate situations, and loving attitudes and dispositions.

basil (page 30)	higuereta
yerba buena/mint (page 32)	jagüey
frescura	sunflowers
watercress	Everclear
canistel	Agua Florida (page 35)
amor seco	32 oz canning jar
mango leaf	

Basil: See page 30.

Yerba buena/mint: See page 32.

Frescura (*Pilea microphylla*): Indigenous to South and Central America, Florida, Mexico, and the West Indies, frescura is used medicinally as a diuretic that supports urinary ailments. It is also an insulin balancer and a supplement providing pancreatic support. Metaphysically, it expels negativity, specifically through the breath, and clears the mind while attracting good fortunes and love into our lives and homes. "Frescura, expel all negativity and negative influences from my life and aid me to return to a state of balance. Spirit of blessings and good fortune, help me to attract love and kindness in all my dealings and interactions, be present within me and my life!"

Watercress (*Nasturtium officinale*): Native to Asia and Europe, watercress is an aquatic, leafy vegetable that is medicinally engaged to treat swollen breathing passages in the lungs, coughs, bronchitis, colds, and flu. As a spiritual medicinal, it attracts the Spirits of the River and creates and sustains flowing energies (versus stagnant). It specifically works with wealth and prosperity, and it helps these energies to flow into our lives. "Spirit of Watercress, whose energies burst through stagnation in all forms, return my natural rhythms and flow, and carry wealth and prosperity back into my life."

Canistel (*Pouteria campechiana*): Indigenous to southern Mexico, Belize, Guatemala, and El Salvador, canistel is medicinally employed to treat conditions such as skin eruptions and abrasions, liver disorders, and epilepsy. As a spiritual ally it attracts victory and success despite any obstacles (and it is a great court case herb). "Canistel, essence that grants success and victory, aid me as I triumphantly claim my blessings in easy and organic ways."

Amor seco (*Meibomia barbata*): Originally from Puerto Rico and the Caribbean, amor seco has medicinal properties that have been utilized to treat asthma and lung disorders, constipation, colic, blood infections, and overall body aches. Known in English as strong back, this botanical attracts romantic energies and ensures that relationships are deeply connected. It has a glamour effect and can increase sexual chemistry. "Spirit of Amor Seco, I call to you to be present in this working. Essence of glamour and bewitchment, help me to accentuate my own beauty and to radiate that beauty in the world. Spirit that awakens and intensifies romantic chemistry, be with me in my relationships and increase the sexual desire of all who see me."

Mango leaf (*Mangifera indica*): Originating in India, mangoes have spread across most tropical and subtropical regions in the world. Medicinally, mango leaves are known to have antiparasitic properties as well as treat kidney and gallbladder stones, lower blood pressure, and improve insulin production and absorption in the body. Spiritually, mango is associated with sweetness, joy, love, commitment, prosperity, and abundance. "Spirit of Mango, help me to sweeten my life and to absorb my blessings, be with me, Mango."

Higuereta, castor bean (*Ricinus communis*): Indigenous to tropical East Africa around Ethiopia, castor bean has been engaged as a laxative to treat constipation, as a form of birth control, and as a treatment for leprosy and syphilis. Metaphysically, it sprouts fortunes, creates fame through word of mouth, and is an extremely powerful blessing herb. "Higuereta, Being of fortune and fame, open the paths for success, bounty, and blessings to come into my life. Spirit of wonder who attracts positive attention and reputation from all corners of the Earth, let my name and accomplishments spread like wildfire throughout community."

Jagüey (*Ficus trigonata*): Native to South, Central, and North America as well as the Caribbean, jagüey has demulcent, emollient, and laxative properties and has been utilized in poultices to ease skin inflammations. As a spiritual ally it attracts good fortune and banishes evil spirits and negativity. It is also employed for tough legal problems because of its dominating and controlling personalities (it wins at all costs). "Spirit of domination and control, Jagüey, assist me in my times of need. Banish all negating forces and assist me as I claim the blessings that are rightfully mine."

Sunflowers (*Helianthus annuus*): Sunflowers attract the light and elevation of the sun into our lives—specifically, the invisible Elders of the day to come bless. "Spirit of Sunflowers, essence of light, grace, and expansion, fill my life with the light of the Cosmos and help me expand into a larger version of myself. Grace my life with joy and sweetness, and guide happiness and contentment to my door."

Curandera's Restoration and Peace Water

This formula can be used as a wash for the crown, back of the neck, and pulse points when you are feeling overwhelmed with anxiety or when tempers are flaring and as well as kept in bottles and placed in every room of the house to create peaceful and calming energies.

anil or blue ball	**yerba mansa**
Florida Water (page 35)	**yerba buena/mint (page 32)**
Everclear	**blessed thistle**
spring water (page 99)	**basil (page 30)**
Peaceful Home Oil (page 125)	**rose (page 26)**
cascara sagrada	**marigold (page 26)**
yerba santa (page 126)	

Anil or blue ball: Similar to a bath bomb, anil or blue ball is an ingredient utilized in Brujería to ward off the evil eye, energetically calm the nervous system, attract blessings and blessed Spirits, and attract luck and good fortune. It is thought to have both protective and victorious properties. "Spirit of Anil, we call to you to be an ally as we attract peace, tranquility, and restoration in our lives. Spirit that protects us against all heating, toxic, and caustic forces, people, and energies, enshroud us in the juiciness of life and help us to be at peace internally and have that reflect in our homes and spaces. Be with us, Spirit of Anil."

Florida Water: See page 26.

Everclear: A 100 proof grain alcohol, Everclear helps extract all the botanical constituents while killing any mold spores or bacteria that could be present on the herbs.

Spring Water: See page 99.

Peaceful Home Oil: See page 125.

Cascara sagrada (*Frangula purshiana*): Native to western North America and southern British Columbia, cascara sagrada acts a purgative and colon cleanse that loosens and increases bowel movements. In peace work it is utilized to calm tensions and bring perspective, and in legal dealings its properties ensure that the law works in our favor with ease and grace. "Cascara Sagrada, we call to you to help us see all perspectives, and we ground ourselves in the knowledge that triggers and our own emotional disturbances can cause us to see things off balance. We ask your assistance to ease all tensions and to help us see clearly and with compassion the matters at hand, Spirit of Cascara Sagrada, be in our hearts, homes, and Spirits."

Yerba santa: See page 126.

Yerba mansa (*Anemopsis californica*): Native to Central and North America, yerba mansa is attracting attention medicinally due to its strong antimicrobial properties that have been shown to treat antibiotic resistant infections like MRSA, strep, and staph pathogens; in respiratory recipes it acts as an expectorant, helping to clear phlegm and mucus. Spiritually, yerba mansa is highly protective and invites gentle and nourishing energies and experiences into our lives. "Spirit of Yerba Mansa, help me to breathe fully and freely no matter the situation or environment. Assist me in expelling any and all stagnant or unhealthy energies, forces, and experiences that have been inhaled in my life. Yerba Mansa, be with me and teach me how to walk gently in the world and be treated with care, concern, and love."

Yerba buena/mint: See page 32.

Blessed thistle (*Cnicus benedictus*): Indigenous to eastern Iran and Turkey, with its range spreading across the Mediterranean, blessed thistle has been employed for appetite and indigestion and to treat colds, cough, cancer, fever, bacterial infections, and diarrhea. Blessed thistle has also been employed as a diuretic for increasing urine output and for promoting the flow of breast milk in new mothers. Spiritually, it is associated with blessings and holiness, and in Brujería traditions it is said to shield us against negativity and intentional curses and jinxes and to bring spiritual help and aid wherever it is worked with or carried. Blessed thistle is also engaged as a very strong protective aid; some practitioners powder the botanical and sprinkle it around their properties as a ward and protective charm against intruders and evil. "Blessed Thistle, help us to bring blessings, peace, restoration, and calm into our bodies, lives, spaces, and homes, and help us to identify any places and situations in which we are not carrying those energies. Spirit of Peace, Compassion, and Grace, assist us in all manners, protect us from harm, and be with us as we strive for cool and peaceful interactions and dealings. Be with us, Blessed Thistle, this day and every day forthwith."

Basil: See page 30.

Rose: See page 26.

Marigold: See page 26.

Chapter 5

PERFUMES ESPIRITUALES

The Art of Spiritual Perfumes

Fragrance creation as a magical art is one the most powerful resources in a Bruja's tool kit. From recalling forgotten memories, to stimulating and reinvigorating our bodies, to the magnetic draw of a lover's pheromones, scent can bypass our conscious awareness and speak to the deepest parts of ourselves. As a magico-spiritual discipline fragrance plays a central part in all formulas and recipes, but sometimes the focus can be centered only on the medicinal or therapeutic qualities, resulting in unpleasant scents. I don't know how many times I have opened a condition oil (magical perfumes created for different conditions in our lives, such as love or wealth) only to be accosted by the smell. While there are certain categories of magical fragrance creation that are meant to be off-putting, other mixtures, like a love oil, should never make us run away.

Mediums

Let's start with the basics. What do you want to use to carry your magics and why? Picking the right medium or carrier has to do with a number of things:

Longevity: This speaks to the time it takes before a recipe turns rancid and the tenacity or lasting power of the scent. Oil-based carriers as a whole go rancid faster, take more botanicals and essential oils to create the profile, and are more costly to make. Prior to Prohibition in the United States, most spiritual and everyday-use perfumes were manufactured in alcohol, and oils were utilized more on an individual basis, usually made from mineral or olive oils, depending on what was readily available. Once Prohibition was passed, commercial perfumers were forced to find new mediums to work through. Eventually perfume houses were able to shift back to alcohol, but the vast majority of spiritual perfumers have continued using oil to the present day.

Deployment: Sometimes we sacrifice the lasting power of the overall scent for the tactile qualities of oils and solids. One of the tricks of the trade among spiritual perfumers centers on the principles of transmission and absorption. Sometimes we want people to physically touch or absorb our concoctions, and because of alcohol's fast evaporation rate after spraying, oils have a longer tactile staying power.

Diffusing throughout the environment: Solids, unlike oils and alcohols, can be used not only on the body but also as a way scenting whole rooms.

Moving from these considerations, let's jump into discussions of the mediums themselves and why I might choose one over the other.

Alcohols: Please trust me on this, don't waste your time or money on vodka or rum if you are working with alcohol. I highly recommend grain, grape, or sugarcane alcohols of 100 proof or higher. I first started with Everclear and the 100 proof rubbing alcohols found in drugstores and pharmacies. Stay away from perfumer's alcohol for a number of reasons, the biggest being the additive (Bitrex), which carries an acrid/burnt smell and ruins the profile.

Oil: The vast majority of spiritual oils on the market are made from grapeseed, jojoba, or fractured coconut oils. I am giving an olive oil–based anointing recipe below, but it won't keep its freshness for more than a month. Grapeseed is the most inexpensive of the three listed above, but it can lay on the skin versus fully absorbing (leaving an oily residue) and is the fastest oil to go rancid. Fractured coconut oil can last a couple of years depending on the fixative used (fixatives help the lasting power of the profile) but can be expensive for bulk fragrance production. Finally, jojoba is a great carrier because it fully absorbs into skin, but it is cost prohibitive for medium to large batches.[6]

Solids: Perfume solids are wax-based fragrances, and making them is a time-consuming and very detailed-oriented process. They also have the least amount of yield for the effort it takes to produce them, as well as the highest material and ingredient costs.

6   Please note that there are some unscrupulous manufacturers who have been known to have contaminants in their oils that cause birth defects. Just because something is "spiritual" doesn't mean it's actually made by spiritual people or contains anything found in nature.

SCENT CLASSIFICATIONS, PROFILES, AND SPIRITUAL CONDITIONS

If you are interested in perfumery, you will need to know the distinctions between perfumes, eau de toilettes, colognes, and waters/splashes/aftershaves. These distinctions are based on the percentages of botanical essences (aromatics) in the carriers. For the sake of our practices, we will be working with Eau de parfum concentrations.

Splash/aftershave: 1–3 percent

Cologne and spiritual water: 2–6 percent

Eau de toilette: 4–8 percent

Eau de parfum: 8–15 percent

Real perfume or extrait (aromatic extract): 15–30 percent

Now that there is an understanding of what makes a cologne distinct from a perfume, wash, or extrait (percentage of aromatics to carrier), let's dive into the families of scent.

★ **Floral:** This family of scents is pretty recognizable; they are predominantly flowery and sweet in their nature: rose, jasmine, and ylang-ylang are all known stars in this category and are seen in many love, attraction, and blessings formulas.

★ **Citrus:** Spotlighting helpers such as lemon, orange, bergamot, mandarin, and yuzu, citrus-based recipes in Brujería are centered on clearing the ways, raising vibrations, opening doors, and sweetening our paths.

★ **Neo-Eastern (formally Oriental):** Don't get me started on perfumery and the history of its nomenclature (who is naming what and their authority to do so). Neo-Eastern profiles have seductive, honeyed, warm, and resinous tones and are often associated with influence, command, domination, authority, and prestige.

★ **Fougère:** Fougères have a green, bottom-of-the-forest-floor smell (the word *fougère* is French for "fern") that's associated with money, passion, lust, grounding, protection, and asserting boundaries.

★ **Chypre:** Similar to fougère's green tones, chypres are mossy, but they have a bit of spice or sweetness to them.

★ **Gourmand:** Gourmands are food- or fruity-scented fragrances that have berry, vanilla, or chocolate aspects.

★ **Aqueous or marine:** These are water or ocean scents usually referenced in peace, reconciliation, and astral travel formulas.

★ **Soliflore:** Soliflores are single-note essences, or bouquets or accords, meant to mimic a single botanical essence. Sometimes due to the biochemical makeup of a plant, the scent is hard to extract. Examples would be violets, gardenias, and some roses.

While there are some obvious correlations between scent families and their metaphysical associations (floral and love work, citrus and road opening), I encourage you to explore some of the most well-known spiritual conditions and how they could be made utilizing each of the scent families.

Types of Spiritual Conditions

★ Beauty, Charm, Elegance, Bewitching

★ Blessings: Self, Property, or Others

★ Peace, Tranquility, Reconciliation

- ★ Cutting, Clearing, Cleansing, and Releasing
- ★ Influence, Controlling, Dominating
- ★ Justice, Legal Matters, Governmental Affairs
- ★ Employment, Money, Gambling
- ★ Love, Fidelity, Sex
- ★ Repelling and Banishing
- ★ Protection, Boundary Setting, Guarding, Safety
- ★ Mastery, Strengthening, Leadership
- ★ Friendship and Community Building
- ★ Gossip and Evil Eye
- ★ Healing and Elevating
- ★ House, Home, and Family
- ★ Psychic Development and Spiritual Awakenings
- ★ Road Opening and Block Busting
- ★ Success and Clarity
- ★ Intention Setting and Visioning

AROMATHERAPY

Outside of the spiritual and scent associations in perfumes, certain botanicals have medicinal compounds that can improve our physical health. Thought to stimulate the limbic and nervous systems when smelled or to carry vitality-improving compounds when absorbed through the skin, essential oil therapies have a number of uses outside of their olfactory associations. Botanicals like rosemary, camphor, and citronella can be pungent and overpowering outside of the context of aromatherapy, but they play essential roles in formulas ranging from skin elasticity support to mosquito repellent.

FORMULATING BASICS

Goal and Intention Setting: What is the goal that you would like to achieve? How does it feel in each of the senses? What manner can be used to achieve that goal? Oftentimes people don't really know what they want, but they want their circumstances to change with a specific condition. Saying your goal is "love" isn't specific enough because there are many types of loveship. The more explicit you can be with the qualities of your love language and how you actually want to invite love into your world affects the formulas and ingredients employed.

Constructing the Formula: With your intentions and qualities in mind, now you are ready to create a personalized recipe suited to your specific circumstances. Identify three to five ingredients that speak to the primary concerns or conditions that are being addressed as well as fragrance family classifications. Please keep in mind that it's not about throwing everything and the kitchen sink into one formula but about harmonizing the energetic accords of the botanical allies and helpers. As part of your formulation work, consider the quantities of each ingredient and make sure that you are showcasing all the elements versus having them compete.

As with all Brujería, make sure to take copious notes on the ingredients used. Who was the supplier that you ordered from, how fresh were the botanicals, were there climatic conditions that might have affected the qualities (floods, droughts, etc.), what form did you buy it in (root, leaf, powder, whole plant, etc.)? For your purposes most of what you will be working with will be cut and sifted, dried plant materials and roots. It's important to use dried materials because fresh botanicals will cause oil-based tinctures and perfumes to turn rancid fast, and the water content in live plants will turn the alcohol cloudy and unusable.

Creating the Bruja's Tincture: Now that you have settled on a recipe and have taken notes, it's time to create the Bruja(e)'s tincture, the energetic and scent base that the fragrance will be built upon. Follow the same process we've already established to create a sacred space and enchant the materials. You will be literally bewitching the perfume with your intents and prayers as you combine the ingredients.

Aging: For oil- and alcohol-based carriers, I age these tinctures for a full lunar cycle or more to extract as much of the medicinal, energetic, and scent qualities of the plants while keeping in mind the longevity of the carriers that are being used. A trick for fixing—or slowing the aging processes of scents that can contribute to them weakening over time—is to use a drop or two of vitamin E or glycerin as stabilizers in the formula. Once these tinctures have sufficiently aged and extracted as many compounds as possible out of the material, filter it out, and now the base is ready for fragrance.

Perfume Creation: Start off with small experimental batches (10–20 ml) to test the profile; you can create several renditions to see what you like and don't like. Often people want to create the "perfect" fragrance from the get-go and forget that this process is about constant evolution and innovation to meet the conditions at hand. A formula might have been optimal for community needs 50 years ago, but does it speak to our current desires? Just because it's old doesn't make it automatically better, and you should remember that these recipes were based on what was immediately available and represent the best thinking of our ancestors in those times.

As part of the scent-creation process, here are a couple of guidelines to keep in mind about how perfumers build their profiles:

★ **Base Notes:** These essences are usually not the flashiest ingredients but have the most staying power. They provide the foundation or the structure of the recipe. In terms of quantities of ingredients used, it is a 3:2:1 ratio, with base notes being the largest amount. Profiles: frankincense, amber, vetiver, oakmoss, and sandalwood.

★ **Heart Notes:** These botanicals are the meat—the flesh and blood—of the scent and give it its full body and flavor. Heart notes are often more expensive (rose absolute can range from $65 to $3,000 an ounce depending on the quality and vintage), and the natural inclination of some beginning practitioners is to heavily reduce their use. This is not a good strategy because the scent goes directly from top to bottom notes within five minutes and can make it seem like the perfumer overly diluted their formula. Profiles: florals like rose, ylang-ylang, and jasmine; resins and spices like styrax, cinnamon, and nutmeg; and herbs like lemongrass and verbena.

★ **Top Notes:** Top notes are the personality or immediate flavor of the perfume. These notes are the first things we smell when fragrances are opened or sprayed, and they have the fastest evaporation times. What makes a base note a base note versus the top note is its evaporation time. Profiles: citrus, some spices, mints, light herbals like sages and tarragon.

Types of Botanical Distillations (Natural Perfumery)

As you move from perfume classifications, scent families, spiritual conditions, and recipe creations, it's important to understand the types of extraction methods used that distinguish an essential oil from an absolute or distillate. These differences can affect whether a botanical essence is considered a top, heart, or bottom note as well as the overall smell of that ingredient. In my practice I have several botanicals that are represented through essential oils, absolutes, and CO_2 distillation because they each have a different quality of the plant that I am trying to express in the formula.

★ **Essential oils:** Botanicals are heated in water, steam is produced, and the resulting oils are separated and captured. A large amount of plant material is needed to extract the oil, and that results in the rarity of the material. It takes 50 pounds of rose petals to distill one ounce of essential oil.

★ **Absolutes:** Absolutes are the most highly concentrated form of aromatic extraction. To produce an absolute, plant materials are washed in a solvent, which removes the oils and creates a concrete (waxy mass). The concrete is dissolved in ethyl alcohol, and then the alcohol is removed, leaving the botanical oil. This form of extract is the most aromatically similar to the living plant materials found in nature.

★ **CO2 extraction:** Similar to absolutes, CO_2 extractions employ pressurized carbon dioxide (CO_2) under low temperatures as the solvent. Using this method, the CO_2 evaporates as a gas, leaving no solvent residue in the oils.

★ **Fractional distillates:** Every ingredient found in the natural world has hundreds of chemical compounds that make up its fragrance profile. Let's take vanilla as an example. The compound that makes vanilla smell like vanilla is a chemical called vanillin, and it's found in freshly mown hay as well as manure. These vanillin molecules are isolated, removed, and combined from a variety of sources to form a concentrated essence of vanillin. These compounds don't have the full body of the natural scent but can be good bases to formulate from.

★ **Isolates:** Isolates are similar to the distillates mentioned above but only come from a single source where the molecule is isolated and extracted from the material.

★ **Enfleurage:** Enfleurage is a process in which a plant material is highly saturated with fat and allowed to set over a period of one to three days. The botanicals are then filtered from the fat, and the resulting pomade is deeply infused with scent. This method of distillation is extremely costly and time-consuming.

★ **Mélange:** These are solid perfumes made from botanicals and usually a combination of beeswax and jojoba oil.

★ **"Natural mimic":** These are accords or combinations of botanicals that can mimic the fragrance of one plant, such as violets, gardenias, or lilac.

Brujes Basics: Stocking the Magical Cupboard

For those who are just getting into scent magics and spiritual perfumery, consider the lists below as essential ingredients for your metaphysical cupboards.

Botanical Distillations

★ **Essential oils, absolutes, CO2 distillations:** Lavender, eucalyptus, mandarin, frankincense, thyme, bergamot, jasmine, rose, vetiver, cinnamon, neroli, pepper, sage, oakmoss, clove, cardamom, lemon, rosemary, lemongrass

Condition Oils and Perfumes

★ **Oils:** Fire Wall of Protection, Road Opener, Peaceful Home, Crown of Success, Uncrossing, Van Van, Obitsu, Look Me Over, Fear Not to Walk Over Evil, Block Busting, Just Judge, Domination, Goofer, Reversing

★ **Perfumes and waters:** Bay Rum, Agua Florida, Kolonia 1800, Agua de Rosas, Lavender Water, Sandalwood Perfume, Kolonia 1800 Vetiver, Lotion Pompeia, Agua de Tobacco, Agua de Violetas

PERSISTENCE OF SCENT

watercolor paper cut into 2-inch strips
frankincense essential oil
jasmine essential oil

bergamot essential oil
3 pipettes or droppers
timer

The goal of this exercise is to test the evaporation times of each botanical in all ways. This process will help you understand why essences are categorized in their families as well as the lasting energetic effects of each element.

1. Take three test strips, and with your pipette or dropper place a single drop of each essential oil on the strips.

2. Let the strips rest for 10 seconds and initially evaluate each using following criteria: How intense is the smell, rated on a scale of 1–10? Does it have a warmth to its profile, or is it cool or cold? Where does the smell hit your palate? What memories does it bring up? How does it make you feel?

3. Set the timer for 5 minutes and reevaluate, except this time bring awareness to how strong the scent is on the strip: Has it lasted? Is it still as vibrant? Does it still trigger the same emotional memories?

4. Set the timer for 20-, 40-, and 60-minute cycles and reevaluate.

BOTANICAL DISTILLATION DIFFERENCES

3 scent strips

jasmine essential oil

jasmine absolute

jasmine CO2 distillation

3 droppers or pipettes

timer

This exercise will help you understand the differences in scent, energy, and stamina of the different distillation methods and will help you expand your ingredient repertoire.

1. Take three test strips, and with your pipette or dropper place a single drop of each botanical on the strips.

2. Let the strips rest for 10 seconds and initially evaluate each using the following criteria: In what ways are they similar and different in scent? How much potency or strength do they have? How much time does it take for them to evaporate physically, emotionally, and energetically?

3. Reevaluate at 20-, 40-, and 60-minute intervals.

Self-Care Oil

grapeseed oil

vitamin E

yerba buena/mint
herb (page 32)

pink rose buds herb (page 41)

frankincense resin (page 54)

flaxseed

chaparral

Mexican elder

rose essential oil (page 41)

yerba buena essential
oil (page 32)

rose geranium oil

sandalwood oil (page 54)

lavender essential
oil (page 41)

Bruja's Tincture

Yerba buena/mint herb: See page 32.

Pink rose buds herb: See page 41.

Frankincense resin: See page 54.

Flaxseed (*Linum usitatissimum*): The earliest archaeological evidence of flax use and cultivation was 30,000 years ago in what is now the Republic of Georgia, but flax seems to be indigenous to most temperate zones throughout the Northern Hemisphere. Medicinally, flax and flaxseed oil have been shown to lower blood cholesterol and blood pressure and to help with asthma, dysphonia, bad cough, and bronchitis. Metaphysically, flax is associated with health and healing, abundance and money, protection and guardianship, and psychic development (building awareness). "Spirit of Flax, we call for your assistance to support our self-care and self-love practices and to bring our attention to the places of healing within us. Spirit that guards and protects, be our champion and help us to create stable, solid, and long-lasting personal boundaries, and support our bravery through this process. Be with us as an ally and be present in this work, Flax."

Chaparral (*Larrea tridentata*): Native species of chaparral range from Central America to the western states of California, New Mexico, Arizona, Texas, and Oregon. Medicinally, chaparral has been engaged by indigenous communities to treat arthritis, bowel cramps, gas, colds, skin lesions, boils, and sores. As a spiritual ally, they are known for their ability to clear and release physical, mental, spiritual, and emotional poisons and toxins (internalized oppressions); and they invite insight, compassionate guidance, and allyship into our lives. "Spirit of Chaparral, great medicine holder that supports and guides us toward our own healing, rejuvenation, and self-care, assist us as we release all toxins and poisons and claim wholeness. Spiritual ally, friend, and guardian, we call for compassionate community and loving guidance and support. Be with us, Chaparral, both in this work and in our hearts."

Mexican elder (*Sambucus mexicanus*): Indigenous to northern and central Mexico, the Sierra Nevada mountain ranges, Baja California, and Texas, Mexican elder has been well known for its medicinal qualities as an immune booster as well as for its help in treating stomach and digestive disorders, fevers, sore throats, coughs, colds, and flu. As a spiritual ally Mexican elder calls us into full participation in life and helps us dissolve fear, reticence, spontaneity, and courage. "Mexican Elder, be present with us and slowly help us dissolve all self-imposed constraints based in fear and timidity. Help us to flourish and thrive in our lives, and guide us toward playfulness, experimentation, spontaneity, and deep participation in the lives we are living and want to create. Mexican Elder, be our ally and our friend."

Scent Profile

Once you are happy with the fragrance, add a drop of vitamin E to stabilize and fix the scent.

Rose essential oil: See page 41.

Yerba buena essential oil: See page 32.

Rose geranium essential oil (*Pelargonium graveolens*): Originally from South Africa, rose geranium has numerous medicinal qualities, including being an antiseptic, anti-inflammatory, astringent, and sedative. In a spiritual context it opens the heart and guides us toward compassionate understanding of our experiences, balances and harmonizes disparate energies and characteristics, and centers our emotional processes versus trying to bypass them. "Rose Geranium, we call to you to assist us as we develop our heart-centered voices and open toward compassionate understanding of our histories and experiences. As we move in processes, guide our energies and help us to release and let all that is not of us or our true selves flow out like the tides. Spirit that fosters our heart wisdoms, be with us and in this work."

Sandalwood essential oil: See page 54.

Lavender essential oil: See page 41.

Peaceful Home Oil

grapeseed oil

vitamin E

rosemary (page 97)

balm of Gilead

basil (page 30)

copal

yerba santa

basil CO2 extraction
(page 118)

bergamot essential
oil (page 37)

ylang-ylang essential
oil (page 66)

labdanum essential
oil (page 65)

Bruja's Tincture

Grapeseed oil: See page 111.

Rosemary: See page 97.

Balm of Gilead (*Populus candicans*): Native to North America, balm of Gilead has been cultivated as a shade tree since the 1790s. As a medicinal helper it has been utilized as a decongestant and stimulant in cough medicines, and its metaphysical associations relate to reconciliation, soothing discord and disharmony in relationships, mending heart hurts, supporting peace, and reminding us why we want to be in relationship with each other (remembering the good times and not focusing on the negative). "Balm of Gilead, healer of hearts, soother of misunderstandings and conflict, be with us, in our homes, spaces, and relationships with one another. Spirit of peace and mender of broken hearts, assist us in reconciling our expectations with the reality of what is, and support us as we compassionately work toward reparations. Balm of Gilead, remind us of the visions of goodness we see in our beloveds, and help us to continue to love and move toward unity. Be with us, Balm of Gilead, and in this work."

Basil: See page 30.

Copal: Copal is the resin of several species of the Burseraceae (torch-wood) family found in tropical and subtropical regions of South and Central America, as well as other resinous botanicals in North and Central America, including Hymenaea, in the legume family; Pinus (pines or pinyons); Jatropha (spurges); and Rhus (sumac). Medicinally engaged to treat skin alignments and joint pain, copal also has anti-septic properties. All copals have the same vibratory energy, and their subtle differences are spoken about below. "Spirit of Copal, holy pro-tector and guardian, we call you forth here in this work. Assist us in strengthening our bodies, Spirits, and willpower, and cleanse all negat-ing forces from ourselves and our spaces. Help us to take flight and move our lives closer to Spirit."

Yerba santa (*Eriodictyon californicum*): Native to California and the Pacific Northwest, yerba santa (meaning "holy herb") is medicinally known for supporting the lungs and treating respiratory conditions, headaches, fever, and muscle strain as well as for wound healing. Spiritually associated with protecting the self and home, yerba santa supports clearing and cleansing workings while establishing and set-ting good boundaries and demarcating spaces. "Yerba Santa, Holy Herb who sanctifies and blesses, we ask that you stand strong with us today and as we cleanse and uplift ourselves and our spaces and support us as we affirm our boundaries both inside and out. Spirit of Yerba Santa, be with us.

Scent Profile

Once you are happy with the fragrance, add a drop of vitamin E to stabilize and fix the scent.

Basil CO2 distillation: See page 118.

Bergamot essential oil: See page 37.

Ylang-ylang essential oil: See page 66.

Labdanum essential oil: See page 65.

Addiction and Recovery Oil

grapeseed oil

vitamin E

mountain mahogany

blue trumpet vine

passionflower

ginseng

ginkgo

dandelion

milk thistle

chamomile (page 98)

frankincense essential oil (page 54)

ylang-ylang essential oil (page 66)

cinnamon essential oil (page 40)

ginger essential oil

rose essential oil (page 41)

grapefruit essential oil

lavender essential oil (page 41)

Bruja's Tincture

Mountain mahogany (*Cercocarpus montanus*): Indigenous to Central and North America, mountain mahogany is known medicinally as a master tonifier and general strength booster in the body, as well as for treating stomach and intestinal complaints and upsets. On an energetic and spiritual level, mountain mahogany has the ability to unlock all the memories and narratives of illness and disease in the body in order to fully release and flush them out of the system. It identifies unseen and hidden connections in the unconscious that can causes us to go back to older lifestyles and patterns of behavior and supports our elevation (seeing things from a higher perspective) in order to fully make long-lasting change. "Spirit of Mountain Mahogany, help us to fully hold with compassion all of our patterns and histories of addictions, and help us to live and write a different narrative for the future. Spirit that lifts and elevates, help us to feel supported, seen, and loved by the Creator and our communities, and aid us in recovering and remembering ourselves and our possibilities in ways we can't even imagine. Spirit of Mountain Mahogany, support our strength, bravery, and courage, and be an ally to us on our roads and paths to recovery."

Blue trumpet vine (*Thunbergia laurifolia*): Originally from the Indomalayan regions, the blue trumpet vine is an antipyretic (reduces fever), supports the treatment of menorrhagia (menstrual bleeding more than seven days), supports skin repair and rejuvenation, and is widely known for its ability to remove poisons from the blood. Its spiritual properties are associated with relieving depression (the energetic crashes that happen after the highs), consistent self-affirmation and self-love, relieving irritations, reminding us of the beauty of the world, and supporting balanced sweetness and gentleness. "Blue Trumpet Vine, assist us as we detoxify all addictions, toxins, and poisons in our bodies, Spirits, and emotions, and aid us as we journey toward recovery. Supporter Spirit that helps to soothe irritations, inflammation, and depression, help us to reclaim ourselves and our happiness and to see beauty and worth both in ourselves and in the world. Blue Trumpet Vine, aid us as we gently and gradually choose different behaviors and actions in our lives, and help us to break the pulls toward old thinking and ways of being. Spirit of balanced, consistent sweetness, be present with us and in our walks in life. Spirit of the Blue Trumpet Vine, be our ally and friend."

Passionflower (*Passiflora incarnata*): Native to the Southern United States, passionflower is medicinally known to aid with anxiety, insomnia, wound healing, and liver support. Metaphysically, it is called on to calm frayed nerves, support relaxation and rest, and foster the ability to handle stress in a balanced and healthy way. "Passionflower, Spirit that soothes and relaxes, assist me as I prioritize rest and self-care. Help me to handle any stresses with ease and grace and release any anxiety and tension that may dwell within my body. Passionflower, support our magics and be with me in this work."

Ginseng (*Panax ginseng*): The *Panax* genus has a variety of ginseng species that are native to Korea, China, and North America, with each having similar medicinal and spiritual properties. As a medicinal, ginseng is a stimulant and immune system and body-wide tonifier, improves focus and concentration (helps with the fuzzy brain syndrome), and regulates and balances blood sugars in the body. In Traditional Chinese Medicine ginseng is considered energetically as the master tonic herb that bestows longevity, health, happiness, success, joy, and love. "Ginseng, master healer and medicine maker, help us to strengthen and tonify our bodies, minds, and Spirits, and share with us your vitality and life force so we can be fully alive and vibrant both in our bodies and in our energies. Assist us as we break free from addiction to feel safe, held, and supported, and support our renewal and recovery every day of our lives. Spirit of Ginseng, be with us in this work."

Ginkgo (*Ginkgo biloba*): Indigenous to China and central Asia, this helper is medicinally worked with to improve blood circulation to the brain and nervous system, to support recall and memory processes, and as a respiratory tonifier. Spiritually, ginkgo is associated with resiliency, stillness, meditative awareness, hope, peace, self-love and affirmation, and balancing and harmonizing dualities. "Spirit of Ginkgo, awaken within us inner awareness and hopefulness, support us as we reoxygenate our bodies and refresh our Spirits, and help us create new behaviors and actions rooted in the longevity of our lives. Spirit of Ginkgo, be with us in this work and in our lives."

Dandelion (*Taraxacum officinale*): Originating in Eurasia, dandelion has been propagated and spread throughout the globe. As a medicinal ally, dandelion is a liver and brain supportive that helps by removing toxins and reestablishing electrolyte balance. It is also known to treat anemia, skin problems, scurvy, blood disorders, and depression. In spiritual contexts dandelion is associated with the enjoyment of the small—everyday occurrences and blessings, happiness, and inner-child play. "Spirit of Dandelion, be with us in our work, and help us to remember to take part in the enjoyment of life. Spirit of play and happiness, assist us in finding meaningful happiness and play no matter the circumstances or conditions. Dandelion, support our detox and help us to find a new balance within us, and remind us of all the possibilities for engaging healthy joy and hope in our lives."

Milk thistle (*Silybum marianum*): Native to the Mediterranean regions, milk thistle is used medicinally as a master supportive for proper liver function and to treat high cholesterol, diabetes, heartburn, upset stomach, gallbladder ailments, and depression. Spiritually, milk thistle is associated with purification rites, exorcising unwanted and uninvited spirits, happiness and vitality boosting, and strengthening and tonifying our Spirits. "Milk Thistle, work with us as we claim victory and success over all addictions and addictive behaviors. Spirit that detoxifies and nourishes, support our processes and feed our bodies as we anchor ourselves in health, vitality, and happiness. Milk Thistle, be our guide, friend, and advocate and help us to embody ourselves fully."

Chamomile: See page 98.

Scent Profile

Once you are happy with the fragrance, add a drop of vitamin E to stabilize and fix the scent.

Frankincense: See page 54.

Ylang-ylang: See page 66.

Cinnamon: See page 40.

Ginger (*Zingiber officinale*): Originally from Southeast Asia, ginger is another botanical that is cultivated worldwide for both culinary and medical purposes. Having numerous properties associated with heart health, like being an anti-inflammatory, antioxidant, antiplatelet, as well as having hypotensive and hypolipidemic effects, ginger is a potent ally for physical and emotional heart health. Spiritually associated with energy, fire, zeal, and zest for life, it is often combined with love and financial abundance herbs to create fast-acting blessings. "Ginger, assist me as I work with our heart health in all ways. Spirit that breaks and releases blood clots and clears away heat and inflammation, help me to remove all irritants and circumstances that create these conditions. Ginger, support my inner fires and energies, and help me to revivify my life."

Rose: See page 26.

Grapefruit (*Citrus paradisi*): A citrus hybrid originating in Barbados during the 1700s, grapefruit is a cross between a sweet orange and a pomelo. Medicinally, grapefruit seed extract has antibiotic and antimicrobial properties, while the juice can lower cholesterol, improve levels of red blood cells, and treat psoriasis. Spiritually, grapefruit is said to support mental clarity, emotional openness, and concentration; restore our own power; and help us feel aligned with our Spirit purpose. "Spirit of Grapefruit, work with us to show vulnerability and openness, and assist us in restoring our own power and self-determination. Spirit of clarity and mental alertness, support these qualities within ourselves, and guide us toward alignment with our true purpose and true selves."

Lavender: See page 41.

Adjusting to a New Disability or Impairment Oil

jojoba oil

vitamin E

chaparral (page 123)

milky oat tops

holy basil

prodigiosa

cedar essential oil

larch tamarack oil

litsea cubeba essential oil

rose essential oil (page 41)

vetiver essential oil

Bruja's Tincture

Jojoba oil (*Simmondsia chinensis*): Jojoba is indigenous to the southwestern United States and Mexico, and when applied to the skin it treats acne, psoriasis, sunburn, and dry, chapped skin. Spiritually, jojoba is associated with embodied wholeness, comfort, ease, and grounded and healthy relationships. "Spirit of Jojoba, be with us as we gracefully, with ease and comfort, seat ourselves fully in the body we have now. Help us to compassionately attend to ourselves and our well-being, and be with us continually as we adjust to our whole selves."

Chaparral: See page 123.

Milky oat tops (*Avena sativa*): Originating from Africa and Eurasia, oats have become a food grain grown in temperate regions throughout the globe. As a medicinal, oats are utilized to treat joint pain and fatigue, are shown to lower high uric acids in the body (which cause gout), assist with detoxing the bloodstream of narcotics, and are utilized for anxiety, trauma, and stress. As a metaphysical ally they work with mellowing and calming our moods, easing anxiety in our Spirits, combating the energetic effects of daily stress, and supporting balanced sleep and restfulness. "Milky Oat Tops, Spirit advocate that soothes our nerves, realigns our systems toward nourishing support, and eases the stressors in our days, be with us as we relaxedly engage our bodies. Help us to adjust to physical, mental, and emotional transitions and to be held in loving security. Assist us as we name our experiences and help us to adjust, ground, and recenter."

Holy basil (*Ocimum tenuiflorum*): Native to the Indian subcontinent, holy basil has antimicrobial, adaptogenic, antidiabetic, hepatoprotective, anti-inflammatory, and anticarcinogenic properties and is known to treat cold and flu, diabetes, headache, fever, stress, upset stomach, and earaches. Metaphysically, its Spirit works to increase our vitality and life force; is a guardian and protector helper; harmonizes our emotional, spiritual, and physical selves; and helps us to see the "holiness" in our everyday experiences. "Holy Basil, great harmonizer of our emotional, spiritual, and physical selves, assists us as we work to balance our hearts, minds, and Spirits. Vitality booster, support and boost our life force and help us to feel protected and secure as we stabilize and fortify ourselves and our environments. Be with us, Holy Basil."

Prodigiosa (*Kalanchoe pinnata*): Originating from Madagascar, prodigiosa is now cultivated in tropical and subtropical regions around the world. It is engaged as a medicinal helper that treats diabetes, helps to dissolve kidney stones, supports the respiratory system, and when applied topically, treats wounds, boils, and insect bites. As a spiritual ally and advocate, prodigiosa is known as a life-everlasting herb that revitalizes and rejuvenates the physical, mental, and emotional bodies and attracts benevolent Spirits and divinities in our lives and homes. "Spirit of Prodigiosa, we invite you into our bodies and lives to support and nourish our vitality and Spirits. Master teacher who attracts benevolent Beings and Divinities into our lives, support us as we adjust, recenter, and love ourselves fully in the bodies we have now. Be with us, Prodigiosa, and aid our elevation and renewal."

Scent Profile

Once you are happy with the fragrance, add a drop of vitamin E to stabilize and fix the scent.

Cedar: A variety of species in the *Cedrus* genus, native to the mountainous regions of the Mediterranean and the Himalayas, along with other similarly aromatic trees in the genera *Calocedrus*, *Thuja*, and *Chamaecyparis*. Cedar is an antimicrobial, antiviral, and antifungal. It also promotes the immune system by boosting white blood cell production and supports the elimination of waste in the system. Spiritually engaged as a protector medicine, it banishes unwanted and uninvited spirits and energies, and attracts good fortune, money, and resilience and invites Divinities and evolved forces to live with us in our homes and spaces. "Cedar, we call you to us today and ask that you work with us in our medicine. Cleansing Spirit that removes all negativity and negative forces seen or unseen, Cedar, be present in our lives and assist us in creating spaces for divinities to reside both internally and in our homes."

Larch tamarack oil (*Larix laricina*): Indigenous to the Pacific Northwest, larch tamarack is an evergreen tree that has been utilized by native communities for generations. Medicinally, larch tamarack is engaged in treatments for jaundice, anemia, rheumatism, colds, and skin ailments and is a tonic, diuretic, and laxative. Spiritually, larch tamarack is seen as the cosmic ladder that connects our consciousness with the Creator's and helps us navigate the inner and outer realms of reality. As a stabilizing Spirit, larch anchors us in our inner core and aids us through large life transitions while helping us to honor who we have been, where we are now, and who we want to become. "Spirit of Larch, great navigator and helper who grounds us in our true core and assists us in all of life's transitions with joy, comfort, and grace, we call to you to be with us and be within us. Larch, great teacher who connects us to all realms of Being, help us to create bridges and build relationships with all those blessed and transcendent seen and unseen Beings, Divinities, and forces and guide us in our journeys."

Litsea cubeba essential oil: Originating from Taiwan, China, and Southeast Asia, *Litsea cubeba* is known as a digestive supporter and treats chills, back pain, and muscle aches. Spiritually, litsea energizes, purifies, balances, and supports embodied joy and passion. "Litsea, assist us in our work as we bring life and vitality into our bodies. Help us to release and purify all negative narratives and associations we have with our health, and support our happiness and full enjoyment of our simple pleasures. Be with us in our walk, Litsea, and support our rejuvenation."

Rose essential oil: See page 41.

Vetiver (*Chrysopogon zizanioides*) essential oil: Vetiver is a bunchgrass similar to lemongrass, citronella, and other aromatic grasses. Vetiver is called on to help treat emotional shock, loss, trauma, disembodiment, anxiety, stress, and lice, and is metaphysically associated with desire, achievement, clarity, purpose, and manifesting from our innermost heart voices. "Vetiver, essence that captivates and intoxicates all that you touch, help us to develop these energies within us and our spaces. Just as you command a room, let our inner alluring nature call forth all that we desire. As we speak these words and burn this blend, we call forth and attract with ease, and grace, all that we name."

Sex Worker's Perfume, Attracting and Keeping Clients

sugarcane alcohol

Jezebel root

orris root

High John root

echinacea root

galangal

cinnamon (page 40)

clove (page 40)

alkanet

alfalfa

sassafras

rose essential oil (page 41)

jasmine essential oil (page 41)

lilac enfleurage

neroli essential oil (page 37)

cinnamon essential oil (page 40)

benzoin essential oil (page 65)

oakmoss essential oil (page 141)

Bruja's Tincture

Sugarcane alcohol: Sugarcane (*Saccharum officinarum*), a tropical grass originating from Asia, has had a long, sordid history in the Americas. Cultivated for its sugar content, sugarcane and its derivatives have been called on to treat hemorrhages, inflammation, jaundice, and urinary infections. As a Spiritual helper sugarcane supports sympathy, wisdom, beauty, grace, love, and lust. "Spirit of Sugarcane, essence of intoxication and bewitchment, help us to attract consistent, sane, and safe clients, and draw them to us like pollinators to sugar. Captivate them with our charms, and beguile them with Spirits, Sugarcane, be present and sweeten our paths."

Jezebel root (*Iris foliosa*): Jezebel root, or Louisiana iris, is indigenous throughout North and Central America. It shares similarities medicinally and spiritually with orris root. "Jezebel Root, we call you forth to this work to attract well-intentioned, docile, and gentle paying customers who will respect and value us at all times. Let them consistently call on us, consistently look for us, and never feel satiated without our presence. Spirit of Jezebel and all uplifted and elevated Sex Workers, we call to you to assist, support, and be with us."

Note: Some workers suggest anointing the Jezebel Root with your sexual fluids to ensure that your clients know your smell and can find you.

Orris root (*Iris germanica* and *Iris pallida*): Orris root is the root of the iris flower, which is indigenous to the temperate climates of the Americas, Asia, and Europe and usually found in dry, semi-arid, and mountainous regions. Medicinally, it is known as a hormone supporter due to its gland-stimulating properties as well as a blood purifier and kidney booster. Outside of its medicinal nature, orris root has been engaged for centuries in perfumery and spiritually is associated with influence, control, beauty, glamour, bewitchment, and grace. "Spirit of Orris Root, essence of influence and control, help us to be fully empowered and in control of our finances. Aid us as we bring awareness to all the places where we can secure our finances, grow our money, and make the wisest decisions with our spending. Spirit of Orris Root, be with us."

High John root (*Ipomoea jalapa*): Native to Mexico and Central America, High John root is well known in Brujería and Hoodoo for its metaphysical associations with strength, domination, power, virility, and cunning energetic personality, and it is not recommended for any medicinal treatments due to its purgative nature (causes extreme vomiting and diarrhea when taken internally). "High John Root, essence of domination, strength, and power, we command our blessings to immediately hear our call and rapidly appear before us. Spirit of magnetic attraction, essence of allurement, let all those who smell this scent be irresistibly compelled to come forth.

Echinacea root (*Echinacea angustifolia*): Native to North America, echinacea as a medicinal supports, strengthens, and boosts the immune system and provides relief from the symptoms of sore throat, cough, and fever. As a spiritual supporter, echinacea is known as Sampson snake root and is associated with strength and the ability to overcome any obstacle or foe, with success and victory, and with respect. "Echinacea, we ask you to lend us your strength as we claim victory and success in our endeavors. Assist us as we attract clients from the four directions, and ensure that they are respectful and treat us with kindness, Spirit of Echinacea, be with us."

Galangal (*Alpinia galanga*): Native to Southeast Asia and the Middle East, galangal has medicinal properties that include anti-inflammatory qualities, curbing motion sickness, aiding in digestion, and assisting with nausea. Metaphysically associated with control, domination, influence, and commands, galangal is said to get people and circumstance "under foot" or under your control. "Galangal, Spirit that softens defenses, opens influence, and supports our balanced control of situations, aid us to open the hearts, minds, bodies, and Spirits of our beloveds. Let them yearn for our touch and caress and have their attention only on us. Spirit of Galangal, assist us to be fully empowered in our sexualities and desires and let them be fully manifested in our romantic partnerships and relationships!"

Cinnamon: See page 40.

Clove: See page 40.

Alkanet (*Batschia canescens*): Indigenous to Pakistan and Mediterranean regions, alkanet has been utilized as a natural purple (purple being the color of royalty) dye for coloring fabrics. In its medicinal functions, alkanet is an antibacterial, antipruritic (relieves itching and irritation), astringent, and vulnerary (helps heal wounds) and treats varicose veins, skin lesions and ulcers, and bed sores. Spiritually associated with royalty, esteem, wealth, luck, and chance, alkanet energetically crowns us with these energies. "Alkanet, Spirit of Sovereignty, Wealth, Esteem, and Good Fortune, assist us as we attract wealth and wealthy clients to our business. Essence of chance and luck, be with us and help us to be lucky in all our dealings, Alkanet, we call to you, be present in this working."

Alfalfa (*Medicago sativa*): Alfalfa is a forage crop utilized for grazing, hay, and silage for cattle, sheep, and other livestock. Medicinally, alfalfa is employed for kidney conditions, for bladder and prostate support, and to increase urine flow. As a spiritual ally, alfalfa attracts abundance, plenty, wealth, and money (for our finances to be as abundant and sustainable as alfalfa). "Spirit of Plenty, Abundance, and Fortunes, Alfalfa, be present in our lives and assist us in attracting wealthy clients who can financially support and nurture us. Help us to be consistently provided for, and let all those who call upon us be generous with their money and prosperity, be with us, Alfalfa."

Sassafras (*Sassafras albidum*): Indigenous to eastern North America and Texas, sassafras has been utilized to flavor root beers and as an ingredient in filé seasoning in Louisiana Creole cuisine. As a medicinal, pure sassafras oil can be extremely toxic, even in small doses (don't worry about working with the loose herb). Spiritually, sassafras is a wealth generator and protector and uncrosses all negative energies around money and wealth. "Spirit of Sassafras, help us to gather wealth and money from all directions and sources, uncross and remove any negativity or negative influences that try to obstruct us from receiving our due, and protect and shield our abundance, prosperity, and money from outside interference or meddling, be present in our work, Sassafras."

Scent Profile

Rose essential oil: See page 41.

Jasmine essential oil: See page 41.

Lilac enfleurage: Native to the Balkan Peninsula, lilac (*Syringa vulgaris*) is such a light-scented flower that it cannot be distilled in essential oil form. All lilac oils are either synthetic or accords (combinations of florals that create the fragrance). As a medicinal lilac is known to lower fevers and help with gastric inflammation, and it is also considered an antiperiodic (stops the recurrence of diseases like malaria). As a spiritual ally lilac assists with expressions of love, passion, joy, and youth. "Spirit of Lilac, bewitch our clients with excitement, exuberance, and passions, and have them express their appreciation and love by being generous with their money and wealth, work with us and be our ally, Spirit of Lilac."

Neroli essential oil: See page 37.

Cinnamon essential oil: See page 40.

Benzoin essential oil: See page 65

Oakmoss (*Evernia prunastri*): Oakmoss is a variety of lichen that grows throughout most temperate zones in the Northern Hemisphere. In herbalism, oakmoss is a helper known to work with stomach and intestinal maladies and is spiritually associated with fertility, lust, abundance, money, and attraction. Because it is a base note (long evaporation time) it represents long-lasting energies—things that stay with us for long periods of time. "Spirit of Oakmoss, we ask you to add longevity and tenacity to our work. As we call our loves, desires, and blessings, help us to keep these near and don't let them slip away. Oakmoss, we call and attract all of our desires to us immediately with your assistance, helper Spirit, we call these blessings forth."

Healing from Abuse Perfume

alcohol base

milky oat tops (page 133)

skullcap

St. John's wort

motherwort

passionflower (page 128)

angelica essential oil

fir balsam essential oil

helichrysum (life everlasting) essential oil

blue tansy essential oil

rose geranium essential oil

Bruja's Tincture

Milky oat tops: See page 133.

Skullcap (*Scutellaria galericulata*): Indigenous across the Northern Hemisphere, skullcap is part of the mint family and has been medicinally employed as a mild relaxant and for use in treating anxiety, nervous tension, and convulsions. Skullcap species in the Americas have been shown to have antioxidant properties that protect against Alzheimer's and Parkinson's. As a spiritual helper, skullcap soothes and calms the energetic bodies and quiets fight-or-flight responses, as well as creating peaceful states of mind and relaxed awareness. "Spirit of Skullcap, assist us as we lean into deep rest and relaxation. Help us to feel secure in our minds, bodies, and Spirits and to neutralize panic, stress, and fear responses. Spirit that works with memory and recall, help us to heal and feel whole again, and help us to not relive in our memories the abuses and suffering of the past. Be with us in this work and in our lives, Skullcap."

St. John's wort (*Hypericum perforatum*): Originating from North Africa, western Asia, and Europe, St. John's wort is medicinally known as a helper for depression, anguish, mental fatigue, and hopelessness. As its scientific name suggests, St. John's wort's spiritual qualities allow us to pierce the mental and emotional fogs and clouds in order to allow the sun into our lives. "St. John's Wort, assist us as we claim our light, joy, and freedom both within our bodies and in our lives. Help us to uplift our moods and Spirits, and help us to feel and see our inner light and radiate joy, love, and healing throughout our bodies and our spaces. Be with us and be present."

Motherwort (*Leonurus cardiaca*): Motherwort is indigenous to central Asia and southeastern Europe, but its cultivation has spread through the Americas and most of the globe. Medicinally, it is employed to treat high blood pressure, irregular heartbeats, heart failure, and anxiety, and it is well known as a uterine stimulant. Metaphysically, it is associated with soothing the emotional heart and promotes gentle courage and bravery through prioritizing nourishment and self-care. "Spirit of Motherwort, calm and soothe our hearts and help us to fully care for ourselves and those we love. Assist us, Motherwort, to decrease hypertension and be steady and strong with our heartbeats.

Spirit of Motherwort, support us as we courageously make changes in our lives to support and love our hearts, bodies, and Spirits."

Passionflower: See page 128.

Scent Profile

Angelica (*Angelica archangelica*) essential oil: Native to northern Europe, Russia, Iceland, Greenland, and the Himalayas, angelica is utilized in medicinal treatments for nervousness and anxiety, fear, trouble sleeping, circulatory issues, dementia, stroke, and muscle and joint pain. Its metaphysical qualities are highly protective and attract the highest guardians (archangels) and defenders to surround us and our homes with loving, compassionate kindness while blocking all negating forces from entering our lives. "Angelica, holy guardian protector, surround us with your wings and protect us against all harm and illnesses. Spirit that cools the nervous system and releases anxiety, fear, and the troubles in the heart, help us to recover ourselves and be renewed inside and out."

Fir balsam (*Abies balsamea*) essential oil: A tree originating in North America, fir balsam has antiseptic properties and creates an analgesic protective covering for burns, bruises, wounds, and sores when applied topically to the skin. As a spiritual ally it helps us energetically rise from distraught and emotional density while tapping into our nourishing root systems. It helps us to identify and expel all the internalized misconceptions that have been swallowed while showing us how to reintegrate safely into the world. "Fir Balsam, Spirit who coats our rawness, relieves our pain, and protects us from further harm, be with us in our work and in our lives. Spirit of integrity, strength, resilience, and peace, help us to stand fully as we are, and help us to reach and rise to the Cosmos."

Helichrysum (life everlasting) essential oil: Helichrysum, or life ever-lasting, is a member of the sunflower and daisy family (Asteraceae) and is known for its anti-inflammatory, antifungal, and antibac-terial properties. Helichrysum comprises various species, most notably *Helichrysum italicum*, that range from the Mediterranean basin to South Africa to Australia. Spiritually, helichrysums work to heal all the places internally that we feel are unhealable; they open the heart and Spirit of illumination and light, heal the scars of past suffering and emotional wounding, and are regarded as a master connector that bridges the self with the creative, blessed, and elevated forces, ener-gies, and Spirits. "Spirit of Life Everlasting, Master Wound Healer, aid us as we identify all emotional, spiritual, and psychic traumas, suffer-ing, and pain, and work with us to compassionately heal and soothe all of these areas, even the ones we think are unhealable. Spirit of con-nection, warmth, and vitality, warm our bodies with your light, spread your ever-lasting vitality within our bodies, and connect us to our true selves, true purposes, and with the Blessed Beings in the Universe. Be with us, Life Everlasting."

Blue tansy (*Tanacetum annuum*) essential oil: Native to Morocco and cultivated across the Mediterranean, blue tansy has found recent fame in the skin-care industry due to its ability to clear congested pores, calm skin inflammation and irritation, reduce heat, kill bacteria that cause pimples, reduce redness, and treat troubled and delicate skin. Metaphysically, blue tansy cools heat and inflammation in the heart and emotional bodies, helps us to affirm our love for ourselves while assisting us in taking actions based upon that love, supports our expansions, and cools anxiety, tension, and stress in the mind. "Spirit of Blue Tansy, help us to kill all negating forces, entities, and beings hiding under our skin, and relieve the pain, inflammation, and irritations that they have caused. Blue Tansy, with your assistance we affirm ourselves fully with love, understanding, kindness, and grace and see the true reflections of who we are. Spirit of Blue Tansy, relieve our pain and protect the delicate parts of ourselves as we expand past all limitations that have been put upon us. Be with us, Blue Tansy, and be present in our hearts, minds, and Spirits."

Cash/Hustle Perfume

High John root (page 138)

echinacea root (page 138)

alkanet (page 139)

alfalfa (page 139)

rue (page 58)

China aster

cinnamon (page 40)

marjoram

sassafras (page 139)

bergamot essential oil (page 37)

neroli essential oil (page 37)

oakmoss essential oil (page 141)

cinnamon essential oil (page 40)

patchouli essential oil

jasmine essential oil (page 41)

ginger essential oil (page 131)

Bruja's Tincture

High John root: See page 138.

Echinacea root: See page 138.

Alkanet: See page 139.

Alfalfa: See page 139.

Rue: See page 58.

China aster (*Callistephus chinensis*): Native to Indochina, Europe, North America, Australia, and New Zealand, China aster has been employed as a medicinal externally to treat headache and nausea. Metaphysically, China aster attracts abundance, prosperity, luck, and chance into our lives. "Spirit of China Aster, come forth and help us to attract financial stability, money, opportunity, and luck in our lives. As we raise our awareness and raise our finances, support and protect our incomes and open the paths to luck, chance, and fortune in our lives, Spirit of China Aster, be present with us continually."

Cinnamon: See page 40.

Marjoram (*Origanum majorana*): Originating from the Middle East, Turkey, Cyprus, and the Mediterranean, marjoram is utilized both as a culinary and a magico-spiritual herb. As a medicinal, marjoram is both a heart and a nerve tonic promoting circulatory health as well as treating coughs, gallbladder conditions, stomach cramps and digestive disorders, depression, dizziness, and migraines. Spiritually, marjoram is associated with wealth, prosperity, and money drawing; promotes grief and sadness relief; and supports joy and happiness throughout our days. "Spirit of Marjoram, be with us in our money work and help us to see possibility and new opportunities as we protect the resources that we have. Spirit of financial awareness, support our awareness and true understanding of where we currently are with our money, and help us to secure and protect our sources of income as we attract and magnetize luck and fortune to ourselves, our businesses, and our homes."

Sassafras: See page 139.

Scent Profile

Bergamot essential oil: See page 37.

Neroli essential oil: See page 37.

Oakmoss essential oil: See page 141.

Cinnamon essential oil: See page 40.

Patchouli (*Pogostemon cablin*) essential oil: Indigenous to Southeast Asia, patchouli is medicinally utilized for relaxation and stress relief while promoting a healthy immune system. Employed externally for dermatitis, acne, and dry, cracked skin, patchouli is also considered a master anti-inflammatory as well as having digestive support and insect-repellent properties. In metaphysics, patchouli is associated with passion, lust, wealth, money, and royalty while aiding with deep concentrative and meditative states. "Patchouli, Spirit of passion, money, wealth, and financial abundance, attract to us financial blessings and abundance. Essence that secures and protects fortunes and increases wealth, money, and financial opportunities, help us to see our roads to being financially secure, wealthy, and prosperous, while helping us to identify all the places where we haven't utilized our money flows to their fullest. Spirit of Patchouli, be with us and our work, and bless us with financial security and abundance."

Jasmine essential oil: See page 41.

Ginger essential oil: See page 131.

To Come Out Loud and Proud! Perfume

alcohol base

helichrysum (life everlasting) (page 144)

damiana

goldenseal

master root

deer's tongue

violet leaf

saffron

yarrow

patchouli essential oil (page 147)

labdanum essential
oil (page 65)

oakmoss essential
oil (page 141)

vanilla essential oil (page 48)

myrrh essential oil

lilac enfleurage (page 140)

jasmine essential
oil (page 41)

yuzu essential oil

bergamot essential
oil (page 37)

Bruja's Tincture

Alcohol base: See page 35.

Helichrysum (life everlasting): See page 144.

Damiana (*Turnera diffusa*): Native to the subtropical regions of southern Texas, Mexico, Central and South America, and the Caribbean, damiana has a rich cultural and medicinal history in Brujería. It is medicinally called on as an ally to treat depression, headaches, upset stomachs, impotence, and constipation. The herb is spiritually associated with connected intimacy, unfiltered sexual expression, connected engagement, divination, meditation, and quieting the inner talkative mind. "Spirit of Damiana, be with us in our work to open our channels, our minds, our hearts to uplifted, compassionate, and caring messages. Help us to distinguish between true insight from illusion and help us to be receptive and discerning. Spirit of Damiana, we call to you, be present with us."

Goldenseal (*Hydrastis canadensis*): Goldenseal is an antibacterial and anti-inflammatory and has immune-boosting qualities, and when applied externally it treats rashes, ulcers, wound infections, itching, eczema, acne, dandruff, ringworm, herpes blisters, and cold sores. Originating in North America, goldenseal has spiritual qualities that include protecting that which we hold most sacred, healing the sores and irritants troubling our emotional states, and attracting positivity in abundance. "Spirit of Goldenseal, protector of our innermost treasures and healer who cools and coats the sorest parts of ourselves, be with us and be our ally as we fully embrace and love our complete selves. Help us to let go of any preconceived notion of who we are supposed to be, and support our full becoming. Goldenseal, surround us in your golden warmth, and seal away all negating, inflammatory, and irritating people, energies, and forces. Be with us, be around us, and be within us, Goldenseal."

Master root, masterwort (*imperatoria ostruthium*): Originating in central Europe and the Mediterranean regions, masterwort is a main ingredient in bitters and liqueurs and is utilized to treat gastrointestinal difficulties, skin rashes and lesions, respiratory infections, fever, flu, and colds. It also has a long history in fumigatory rites and incense blends. Metaphysically, masterwort is associated with strengthening our will and resolve, calming our emotional responses, protecting all aspects of ourselves and integrating disparate parts of our psyches, and being in full mastery of ourselves and how we walk in the world. Some elders say that grinding the full root to powder and then sprinkling it will cause Spirits to manifest before us. "Master Root, help us to fully sit in our power, value, worth, and esteem, and help us to be strong in ourselves and the lives we build. Spirit that calms and cools our responses, help us to deactivate triggers and trauma narratives and reverse all negating energies and people who cannot see us for who we are. Master Root, we call to you to bring forth all the courageous, uplifted, and transcendent LGBTQI Ancestors and remind us continually of their presence, strength, courage, and love. Be with us, Master Root."

Deer's tongue, vanillaleaf (*Carphephorus odoratissimus*): Its leaves have demulcent, diaphoretic (sweat-inducing), and diuretic properties, and it was once employed for treatments of malaria and other parasitic infections. This botanical contains coumarin (the chemical compounds that give it its vanilla-like smell), but when taken internally it can damage the liver and over-thin the blood. Native to the coastal regions of North and Central America, deer's tongue been utilized spiritually for its intoxicating and bewitching smell, to attract lovers and have toe-curling sex (if you can't tell I'm a big fan). Deer's tongue is also a big advocate for getting people to speak what is on their mind and communicate from the heart (to have them open their mouths and tell you how they really feel). "Deer's Tongue, support us as we celebrate who we are and express with openness and vulnerability our experiences. Spirit of intoxication, allurement, and bewitchment, be with us as we fully bloom in ourselves and intoxicate the world with our energies. Support us, Deer's Tongue, and give courage and strength to all of us who go after ourselves, our joy, our dreams, and the lives we want to live. Be with us, Deer's Tongue, and be present in this work."

Violet leaf (*Viola odorata*): Native to temperate zones throughout the Americas and the globe, violets have been employed in cooking, perfumery, and medicine making since antiquity. Violets have cooling, soothing, and anti-inflammatory properties and are used to treat dry skin, abrasions, insect bites, eczema, varicose veins, and hemorrhoids. Spiritually, violet draws and attracts love and loving experiences and is a heart protector against bigoted language and hate-filled remarks. Violet calls us into peaceful serenity and heals the abrasiveness of the world (it is also great for amplifying lusting energies in others—but you didn't hear it from me). "Spirit of Violet, protector of the heart, be with us as we stand against bigotry and hate-filled people and forces. Help us to be tender and loving to ourselves, our families, and our communities and to attract loving experiences and peoples to ourselves, our spaces, and our homes. Spirit of Violet, be with us always."

Saffron (*Crocus sativus*): Saffron is the flower threads collected from the saffron crocus. It is employed as a spice and a dye and has a deep religious and spiritual history within the traditions birthed on the Indian subcontinent. Indigenous to the Mediterranean region, Asia Minor, and Iran, saffron is employed medicinally to treat depression and anxiety, improve memory function and recall, and relieve menstrual cramps, and it is also a mild expectorant and antitussive (cough suppressant). Metaphysically, saffron speaks to the value we place on ourselves and the ways in which we show that value to the world. Saffron is an aphrodisiac and creates emotional bonding between partners. "Spirit of Saffron, sovereign of self-worth and self-affirmation, help us to see ourselves fully and without artifice for who we are and the beauty we hold. Spirit of connected interactions and emotional empathy, help us to recognize our own humanity and the humanity of others as we move throughout our lives. Saffron, be with us, be present in our work, and sit in our hearts."

Yarrow (Achillea millefolium): Native to North America, Asia, and Europe, yarrow supports mental clarity and emotional balance, and helps to treat liver and skin ailments, asthma, cold and flu, digestive inflammation, and diarrhea. Spiritually, yarrow is associated with physical and psychic protection. This helper has a long history of connection with divination and being able to open the doors to Spirit while staying grounded and centered in ourselves. "Spirit of Yarrow, great helper and friend of humanity, walk with us. Yarrow, we call to you to cleanse us and our spaces of all obstacles, challenges, and low-level energies. Help us to remove all anxiety and depression, and support us as we stand in our clarity and truth. Open the doors to the Divinities and our transcendent ancestral courts, and let us be present to their advice and messages."

Scent Profile

Patchouli essential oil: See page 147.

Labdanum essential oil: See page 65.

Oakmoss essential oil: See page 141.

Vanilla essential oil: See page 48.

Myrrh (*Commiphora myrrha*): Several trees in the Burseraceae family are cultivated as a source for myrrh. It is one of the most easily recognizable of the resins due to its long history of use, from ancient Egyptians to the modern-day Catholic Church. Native to the Arabian Peninsula and North Africa, myrrh has been employed since antiquity as an antibacterial agent, antifungal, astringent, antiseptic, antiparasitic, cough suppressant, and antispasmodic as well as to stimulate menstrual flow. In its spiritual aspects, myrrh is associated with the Divine Feminine and is called on so we can hear and receive the voice of Divinities; it is also a calming and soothing force for our Spirits. "Myrrh, Spirit of the Divine Feminine in all her forms, we call to you to be with us in our work. Assist us as we soothe and calm our energies, our hearts, our Spirits, and our spaces, and help us to become aware of the voices of the Divine within ourselves that are leading us toward our liberation. Spirit of Myrrh, be with us as we elevate."

Lilac enfleurage: See page 140.

Jasmine essential oil: See page 41.

Yuzu (*Citrus junos*) essential oil: Originating from China and spreading across Korea and Japan, yuzu is a hybrid of mandarin orange and *Citrus cavaleriei*. Yuzu has powerful antioxidant properties due to vitamin C and limonene, neutralizing agents that capture free radicals and reduce inflammation. Like all citruses, yuzu cuts and clears any blockages or obstructions from our paths and sweetens our ways. It helps with calming anxiety, nourishes and strengthens our nerves and nervous systems, relieves pain, and improves recovery time after health and emotional challenges. "Spirit of Yuzu, opener of the ways and sweetener of our paths, assist us as we joyfully express who we are and how we love and inhabit our bodies. Spirit who nourishes and strengthens our nerves, relieves our pains and burdens, and supports our immediate recovery from challenges, be with us as we claim ourselves fully and celebrate all of our unique differences."

Bergamot essential oil: See page 37.

Chapter 6

VELAS Y LUCES ESPIRITUALES

The Arts of Ceremonial Light Setting

Light as a life-giving and vitality-supporting force, as a symbol of clarity and our ability to envision and see, as well as a representation of energy, fuel, expansiveness, and inner illumination, are all qualities present in spiritual candle workings. As we journey together in this chapter, we will delve into different forms, methods, and recipes utilized for upliftment, protection, and blessings for ourselves and our loved ones.

Candle Colors and Their Meanings

White: Illumination, inward progression, ascension, blessings, peace, harmony, healing, soothing and calming energies, reflection of negativity, purification, protection, clarity of mind and purpose.

Red: Passion, energy, action-oriented behaviors, protection, warriorship, vitality, strength, desire, groundedness, powers of the blood, luck, sexual intimacy, and romantic love.

Orange: Road opening, creativity, fertility, spontaneity, mutability, flexibility, divinatory visions/omens/dreams, breaking addictions.

Yellow: Willpower, breaking addictions, strength, intention setting and devotional practices, treasures, gifts, financial prosperity, joy, happiness, positive attitude, solar energy, attracting blessings and good Spirits, friendship, community development and involvement.

Green: Money, wealth, having resources and food on the table, abundant harvest, consistent employment and work, victory and success in business ventures, wisdom of the heart, balanced connection with self and others.

Blue: Restoration, compassion, kindness, generosity, nourishment, healing, trust, fidelity, insight, perception, invisible transmissions and communications, astral travel in dreams, the mystery or unseen nature of existence.

Purple: Royalty, sovereignty, mastery, success, ambition, dominance, connection with high realms, enlightened messages, prophetic dreaming, visionary experiences, leadership.

Pink: First love, crushes, reconciliation, friendship crushes, sobriety, emotional connections, physical intimacy, daydreaming, healing, softening, sweetening

Black: Reversing, expelling, repulsing, negative intentions, expressions of deep grief and worth matters, witchcraft, pain, negative forces, banishing.

Brown: Legal matters, court dealings, contract signing, issues with law, immigration, governmental agencies and judges, adjudication and arbitration.

Gold: Lucky hands and gambler's luck, making money hand over fist (striking it rich), power, control, having things at our fingertips, owning and amassing wealth, pleasure.

Silver: Spirituality, moon and lunar associations, water, mercurial energies, psychic talents and development, emotional strength and fortitude, sensing the unseen.

Red over Black "Love Uncrossing and Reversing" Candle: This combination is considered a double action candle, which means it does two things at once. The red unblocks our romantic lives, and the black returns things to their source.

White over Black "Purifying and Healing and Reversing" Candle: In this combination the white addresses purifying, healing, and protecting the self, and the black returns all negative forces to their origination.

Green over Black "Financial Cleansing and Reversing" Candle: In this form the green represents the cleansing of financial hardships, bad luck, and blockages, and the black reverses these things back to their sender.

Black over Red "Reversing" Candle: This is a universal reversing light that returns all negating energies and forces back to their sources.

Divining the Remains:
The Art of Candle Reading

Part of being a master in any craft is the presence and awareness that is required to refine the art. Candle burning, like other ephemeral crafts, is more than just lighting it and leaving it to burn. The candle becomes a medium and conduit through which the spell or offering is energetically channeled. As we become aligned to the subtle energetic movements in this process, divinatory signs and omens are often communicated throughout the burn. It's a snapshot of an energetic moment, a brief moment where creation is responding to our workings. As with all forms of divinatory experience, we can become hyper-aware and distort everything into a sign or omen. More often than most practitioners like to admit, the quality of their candles is substandard because as a whole, manufactured witchcraft and Brujería products are treated as afterthoughts.

How can we read candles knowing this information? Discernment and common sense play vital roles within these practices because you have to be aware in this reality before you start to work with any other one. If you notice that the wick is skewed off to one side, the wax is already melted in the candle before the purchase, the candle is covered in a thick layer of dust and grime, all of the signs point to bad burns.

Again, use this information as a guide for suggestive meanings versus the absolute "truth." I encourage everyone to further research their family, community, regional, and cultural interpretations of signs and symbols.

Keeping all this in mind, below are some general patterns that I have seen throughout the years and the meanings I have picked up from both teachers and personal associations. (The Universe will speak to you in the signs that you know.) Before you start to interpret the outside signs of the candle, sit with how it feels energetically, emotionally, and intuitively; try to sense the emanating Spirit that is speaking out through the images.

Quality of the Burn

Clean Burns: For glass-encased candles, a clean burn is when there are no marks or residues on the glass or bottom of the container. It's similar for stand-alone candles, with little to no wax or herbal remains after completion of the burn. Meaning: Favorable outcomes, things being in alignment with your petition and intention, manifestation of your desire.

Haze or Soot on Glass:

★ **White to Gray:** Slight confusion, lack of focus, clarity-related issues that might be obscuring the information or results that we are seeking, a general sense that we are going in the right direction but that there are scattered energies, anxiety, feeling off.

★ **Dark Gray:** Resistance, blockages, and feelings of constraint or limitation of possibilities and circumstances.

★ **Black:** Intense resistance to the intention or petition, oppositional energies, negativity surrounding the situation, possibilities of not achieving the goal. Consider doing some clearing and cleansing work to break through these circumstances and try this working again.

★ **Herbal Residues:** They suggest that there are people, energies, and circumstances that are physical blocks, literally blocking the way. These residues represent things that are willing to be transformed or attachments that are impairing forward progress.

★ **Glitter or Other Items:** In terms of divination, leftover glitter indicates distractions or issues with concentration, literally being distracted by the shiny-shiny of the world. (I am not a big fan of glitter in candles because it can easily become attached to the wick and cause a horrible burn.)

Flame Pops and Sizzles: Represents Spirit or our ancestral lineages being present in the room and hearing our petitions.

Flame Rises and Falls: The person or persons who are the targets of the work unconsciously sensing what is happening. There can be some partial or slight resistance coming from the person involved, and further divination is required to understand this in the context of the whole burn.

Flame Self-Extinguishes: Strong oppositional energies representing people or forces fighting the working and literally "putting out your light." I would do some strong block buster work and try it again.

Flame Is Drowned: Not having the resources, stamina, or physical energy to complete the task, as well as feeling "drowned" by the labor necessary to transform the circumstances.

Shapes in the Puddles of Wax: Often shapes form in the puddles of leftover wax, and these can be physical images of how things are standing in the work. Hearts, faces, keys, blades, and money are all common figures in burns, and the positioning and condition of the symbol can give us further clues about the meaning.

Streams of Wax: In stand-alone candles the wax can start to flow, and depending on its direction, these streams can be "read." If it flows toward the petition, photos, or objects related to the goal, these signs are positive; if it flows away or visually dissects these items, it indicates some negativity or things flowing in a negative direction.

Emitting Sooty Smoke, Stand-Alone: Unseen or unacknowledged forces acting in opposition to the desire.

Cracks and Breakages: Can be an indication that the candle took the "hit" or blocked something negative that was about to happen. It usually signifies the need to pull back, readjust, and strategize about other ways of achieving the goal.

Locations on the Candle

Top: When signs occur at the tops of the candles, they can point to issues with the physical, mental, emotional, and spiritual head or our consciousness. Sometimes it represents past situations or circumstances that we are transcending, as well as what is at the surface or what's at the visual top of situations. Sensory perception of things.

Middle: Signs in the middle of a burn or remains left in the middle of glass-encased candles represent tense communication, things currently happening. It can also point to circumstances happening in the middle of our bodies (chest, heart, lungs, etc.). Inward perception, gut instincts, and intuitive knowing.

Bottom: Represents what is at the root or bottom of the situation and can also indicate where things are headed. When remnants of the burn appear at the bottom, this points to issues from the past that are following us into the present and future—patterns, behaviors, addictions, or constraints that are shaping the way we see the world. If this is a health-related petition, look for circumstances with feet or legs (injuries, edema, parasites, etc.). Foundation for the ways that we know, sense, and intuitively feel and view the world and our environment.

Front: Circumstances happening in front of us that we are fully aware of and engaging. Things happening in the foreground. A rounder interpretation of the sign will depend on where on the front of the candle (top, middle, bottom, or sides) it is appearing.

Back: Unconscious or unseen circumstances, or circumstances happening outside our perceptions or understandings, that are playing a role in our petitions. Things happening in the background.

Right Side: Actions, behaviors, or energies we are sending out that are involved in the circumstances. Paternal lineages, solar associations, yang qualities (hollow organs like stomach, intestines, gallbladder, and bladder).

Left Side: Thought patterns, self-talk, emotional experiences, the inner world and our processes. Maternal lineages, moon associations, yin qualities (solid organs like heart, lungs, liver, and spleen).

PROCEDURES FOR CANDLES

This is the order I use for glass-encased candles; the inscribing and loading steps are reversed for stand-alone candles. For reversing work, an extra step is added before loading, butting the candle (digging out the end of the wick at the bottom and using that end as the top of the candle).

Cleansing and Honoring

Please reference "Procedures for All Recipes, Spells, and Rituals in the Book" (page 16) in chapter 1 for the full procedure.

Petition Writing

A petition is a written intention or prayer that unifies the ingredients and gives voice to the goal of the working. There are many types and variations of petition writing in Brujería, and the form that is mentioned below can be employed universally. If you want to get really fancy, make a collage of images that represent the goal and write the text over it.

Things to keep in mind:

★ What is the goal or focus of the work?

★ Write from the heart with simple, clear language.

★ Use action-oriented versus passive language.

★ Keep things short and to the point (one paragraph max).

Narrative Petition

As the name implies, this form of petition writing is about creating a simple story of what you want to achieve as a result of the working. Brujas go about this by creating an elegant sentence that sums up the totality of the desire and then repeating this sentence an odd number of times: 3, 5, 7, or 9.

★ 3 opens possibilities, steps out of the crossroads, communicates to Divinities what is in our hearts.

★ 5 is a manifestation number, the ability to speak things into being.

★ 7 is a spiritual harmonizing number aligning intuitive knowing with conscious awareness.

★ 9 opens the gates of the marketplace, commerce, and dramatic change.

Write a paragraph with an odd number of lines, up to 9, speaking toward the goal.

Next, write your full name (the way you currently identify yourself) in lines diagonally from the upper right corner of the paper to the bottom left, crisscrossing the text you just created. This signifies your active participation in creating the change you are seeking, as well as steering and navigating the energies where they need to go (taking control of the situation).

Now you can draw symbols or sigils representing your desire (hearts for love, dollar signs for money, etc.) in each of the four corners with their directions pointing toward the middle or center of the paper, literally bringing the energies from the four corners of the world into the work.

Some Brujas like to sprinkle a pinch of the herbal mixture they use to load and fix their candles into the center of the paper and anoint the four corners and center of the paper with condition oils appropriate for the goal.

The petition can now be folded either toward you (to attract forces into your life) or away from you (to banish or repel energies) three times, which symbolizes stepping into a new possibility, road, or direction. Finally, the petition can be attached to the candle or placed under it while it burns.

This form of petition writing can also be inserted into charms or medicine bags, pinned into clothing, worn in the shoe, or even inserted into the pillowcase for a good night's sleep.

Fixing and Loading

Fixing or loading refers to the steps that are taken for adding herbal ingredients, powders, and oils to an item, and specifically candles in this section. As a part of each working I will be addressing how to individually fix and load the candles for the appropriate spell.

Inscribing Sigils and Symbols

After the loads are added, you can carve symbols and sigils into the wax (stand-alone candles) or draw them onto the glass with markers, tempura paint, or other materials. The reason why you do it in this order is that if you inscribe or draw first, chances are that things will be smudged or wiped away once things are fixed.

Final Anointings

Sometimes Brujas like to further anoint the candles with a drop or two of oil and rub any remaining herbs on the candle if it's the stand-alone type, or sprinkle them on top if it's glass-encased.

Charging/Praying

After all this work, don't forget to pray over the candle, give it its instructions and repeat the petition, spit into the candle, and blow three times to bring it to life.

Sealing and Knocking

As a way of completing the rite and indicating that the candle is complete, charged, and fully alive, gently knock it three times on the floor or any hard surface (table, desk, etc.) nearby.

Wick Trimming

I can't stress enough how essential it is to trim your wick because it greatly affects the burn. This helps draw the wax up the wick evenly; plus, 80 percent of soot issues can be avoided if the wick is attended to and trimmed regularly. Keep these trimmings because you can reuse them if you ever have to rewick a bad candle.

Lighting and Spending Time with the Work

You just spent a sizable amount of time creating the spell, and this next step becomes the undoing of most practitioners. You actually have to not just light the candle but spend time meditating with it, speaking to, praying over it, even playing music and dancing. Any way that you can relate to the work and bring it into your life will make it more effective and give it a real chance of manifesting your desire.

Extinguishing and Returning Back to the Work

Try to have the candle burning in segments at least three to four hours at a time. This ensures a successful physical burn and also gives it time to energetically unfurl and grow. When you need to extinguish the flame, snuff it or deplete it of oxygen by covering the opening with a saucer or glass, symbolizing that the spell is not finished and that you can return to it. If you forget and accidentally blow it out, don't fret—I have done it a time or 15 and it doesn't dramatically affect the work.

Rewicking

Due to quality as well as the energetic temperament of burns, the candle can have a hard time staying lit. For those instances rewicking is a useful trick, especially after spending this much time enchanting it. Using the wick trimmings and a skewer or other pointy device, create a hole next to the original wick and carefully place a single trimming next to it. Try to make sure that the secondary wick is stable and well situated or it will just fall over and be of no use.

Anima Sola Candle Working (Ecuador Inspired): Freedom from Emotional Purgatory, PTSD Support

The goal of this working is to identify and release past trauma recordings while supporting the inner healing journey. The herbal load is from an Ecuadorian Curandera who works primarily with soul loss and recovery in migrant communities. The seven herbs that she works with are hard to find in the United States, and I have only included the three most accessible outside of Ecuador. These are also hard to find fresh in the States for direct-on-the-body limpia purposes, as was the intent of the original herbal broom, and I have been given permission to modify the formula for my work. Note: If these herbs are hard to find in your area, please see the Healing from Abuse Perfume recipe on page 141 for botanicals with similar correspondences.

Anima Sola glass-encased candle

Agua Florida (page 26)

chilca

pumin

capuli

devil's shoestring

hibiscus leaves

prodigiosa (page 52)

frescura (page 103)

petition

Healing from Abuse Perfume (page 141)

butter knife

small plate or tray

Anima Sola glass-encased candle: Represents our desire to be released from all of our traumas, hurts, and triggers and all behaviors that keep us isolated from our healing resources and communities. The image on the candle is of a solitary woman engulfed in flames and enchained crying out for help and release.

Agua Florida: Used to physically and spiritually clean the candle and our implements.

Chilca (*Baccharis latifolia*): Native to Ecuador, Bolivia, Argentina, Columbia, Peru, Uruguay, and Chile, chilca has amazing anti-inflammatory properties when engaged externally (Elders would crush the leaves, make a poultice, and apply it topically to sites of bone fractures to help pull the inflammation out and support the rebuilding of the bone). Chilca has also been engaged for consistent diarrhea and extreme digestive cramping. In limpias, branches of the plant are cut and added to several other botanicals to create a medicinal broom, which is utilized to sweep the body and remove illness and negative conditions. Chilca treats mal aire (bad or evil air, negative environmental conditions similar to miasma), espanto or susto (grave shock, or the feeling that we are disembodied due to tragedy and trauma), and mal prójimo (being intentionally targeted and abused by our "neighbors" or those closest to us). "Chilca, Spirit of deep soul healing and recovery, help us to break all constraints and chains that keep us locked away in the dark. Healer Spirit, support us in liberating ourselves from all old tape recordings of traumas, and help us to stop reliving the memories of abuse. Great Helper Spirit that reanimates our Spirits and breathes life back into our bodies, be with us and attract to us the resources we need for our full recovery and healing."

Pumin (*Minthostachys mollis*): Similar to chilca, pumin originates in South America, and indigenous communities have utilized it medicinally for the treatment of lung ailments like cough and bronchitis; for stomach ulcers, gastritis, digestive cramping, and headaches; and as an antiparasitic and carminative (herb that relieves gas) for digestive support. Spiritually, pumin clears holes in our energetic auras caused by mal aire, helps us to come back into our bodies after great shock and loss, and helps us to identify unconscious cyclical behaviors.

"Spirit of Pumin, support us as we claim complete health and victory over all that troubles us. Help us to connect back into ourselves, our lives, and our communities, and seal and strengthen our energetic fields and auras. Spirit of Pumin, assist us as we identify cyclical behaviors, and help us to make conscious choices that will move us forward in our elevation. Be with us, Pumin."

Capuli (*Prunus serotina*): Indigenous to South and Central America and eastern North America, capuli is also known as wild cherry or black cherry and has expectorant and mild sedative properties. As an herbal infusion, it has been utilized to treat fevers, colds, and sore throats and to ease the pain of the early stages of childbirth. As a spiritual helper, capuli unifies spiritual, mental, and emotional dualities, attracts light and illumination into the dark corners of our minds and Spirits, and represents longevity and immortality. "Capuli, help us to reclaim our wholeness, and assist us in unifying all parts of Spirits and consciousness as we move toward complete restoration. Spirit of illumination and light, come forth into our Beings and shine into the deepest parts of ourselves, guide us as we empower and embody the fullness of who we are. Spirit of Capuli, soothe our nerves and calm our hearts, be our ally in this work and continually be with us."

Devil's shoestring (*Viburnum alnifolium*): Originating in North America, devil's shoestring is a ground cover shrub with medicinal properties that relieve cramps, muscle spasms, and menstrual cramping. It is also a kidney stimulant utilized for conditions involving pain and spasms. Metaphysically, devil's shoestring ties up all negativity and "devils" that are troubling us or blocking our way (imagine a strangling bush that wraps around evil and binds it). "Devil's Shoestring, bind and capture all evil, negativity, and negative impulses in ourselves, our homes, and our spaces. Spirit that protects and guards, guard our doorways and thresholds and remove all blockages, obstacles,

THE MODERN ART OF BRUJERIA

and stagnant energies that try to impede us from our wholeness and beauty. Be with us, Devil's Shoestring, and continually be present and strong in our lives."

Hibiscus (genus Hibiscus): Indigenous to temperate, tropical, and subtropical regions throughout the world, the edible varieties Hibiscus roselle or Hibiscus sabdariffa are the most commonly employed botanicals in cooking and Brujería. Known to help lower body temperature and treat high blood pressure and diabetes, hibiscus leaves have astringent and demulcent properties. The flower is metaphysically associated with intimacy, sensuality, deep connections, and lust, while the leaves are employed in exorcism and banishing ceremonies. "Spirit of Hibiscus, flower of desire, connection, intimacy, and physical pleasure, we seek your assistance to call all these energies forth with speed and immediacy. With your potent color that dyes everything it touches, touch the hearts, hook the Spirits, and attract to us the blessings we call forth. Spirit of Hibiscus, be present in our work."

Prodigiosa: See page 52.

Frescura: See page 103.

Healing from Abuse Perfume: Utilized here as an energetic support for healing instances of abuse, violence, and emotional trauma.

Procedure

1. Thoroughly clean the candle and your implements.

2. Sealing: Anoint the plate with your perfume in each of the four corners while verbally praying and speaking the petition.

3. Petition writing: Following the instructions on page 161, write a petition and then place it in the middle of the plate.

4. Creating the load: Mix the botanical ingredients together, use a little splash of the perfume to get everything slightly moist, and then verbally pray and speak aloud your petition.

5. Loading: Using the butter knife, carefully carve out a pocket where you can place the load (I usually dig 2 inches down and 2 inches across to create this pocket). Next, add the mixture, then another small splash of the perfume, pray and speak your petition aloud, and finally, place the carved-out wax back into the candle. Finally, you will pray and speak your petition one final time, breathe three times into the candle, knock it three times (tapping against the floor or a hard surface to unify your desires and seal the magics in the candle), trim the wick, and place the candle on the petition paper in the middle of the plate.

6. Lighting: Now you are ready to light the candle and again pray and verbally speak your petition and intentions aloud while visualizing the light of the candle being absorbed into your consciousness and Spirit. As part of this process, you are imagining the light guiding you back to a sense of security, safety, and wholeness. Remember when extinguishing the flame to snuff it out.

7. Disposal: Once it is finished burning, thank the candle, clean out any residues from the burn, and recycle it along with the petition paper.

Citizenship Application Approval Lamp

oil lamp

Agua Florida (page 26)

cascara sagrada (page 106)

galangal (page 138)

High John root (page 138)

Solomon's seal

deer's tongue (page 149)

Low John root

petition

olive oil (page 175)

lamp fuel

Oil lamp: Some of the earliest civilizations produced light from lamps over the millennia and as a result, magico-spiritual traditions and associations were created to utilize them. Popular substances that lamps can be fueled by include oil, kerosene, butter, lard, vegetable oils, and pretty much any type of flammable liquid material.

Cascara sagrada: See page 106.

Galangal: See page 138.

High John root: See page 138.

Solomon's seal (*Polygonatum biflorum*): Indigenous to most of the Northern Hemisphere, Solomon's seal has astringent and anti-inflammatory qualities (really great for muscle and connective tissue support due to repetitive activities—conditions like carpal tunnel or tennis elbow); as a medicinal helper it treats lung and respiratory infections, and applied topically it treats bruises, ulcers, boils, hemorrhoids, skin redness, and edema (water retention). Spiritually, Solomon's seal connects us to enlightened wisdom and brings allies to our aid. When working in legal matters, Solomon's seal attracts victory and success while aligning the court systems with our desires. "Spirit of Solomon's Seal, aid us in our time of need and support our victory and success. Spirit of wise counsel, discernment, and wisdom, help us to embody these qualities, and be crowned with the answers to any questions asked and the full knowledge needed to successfully complete the process. Be with us, Solomon's Seal, as we empower ourselves with the resources needed to win."

Deer's tongue: See page 149.

Low John root (*Trillium pendulum*): All Trillium species originated in North America and Asia; this specific variety has been utilized to treat postpartum uterine bleeding, and when applied topically it staunches external bleeding and provides relief from insect bites. Spiritually, Low John root is associated with victory and success in legal matters and is a dominating herb that take commands of the situation. "Spirit of Low John, assist us as we take command of this process, and help us claim swift victory and success in all matters. Master Spirit of all legal and governmental matters, bring to us supporters who can guide us through the process, and help us convince all those who read these documents to grant our petitions and requests. Be with us, Low John, and aid us in this process."

Olive oil: See page 175.

Lamp fuel: Used as the fuel source to produce light; as with all substances in magic, this too can be prayed over and charged with your intents.

1. Clean the outside and inside of the oil lamp and glass covering and let dry.

2. Petition writing: Using a printed-out copy of all the legal paperwork, write the petition, verbally pray and recite the desire, anoint the application with olive oil in each of the four corners and the middle to seal the intention into the document. This is placed under the lamp while it burns.

3. Loading: Add each of the botanicals one by one into the lamp base and verbally pray and recite your petition. Next, pray over the fuel and fill it to the top. Finally, once all the material and fuel have been added, recite the petition and prayer once more and seal the lamp.

4. Lighting: Before initially lighting the lamp, make sure the petition paper is underneath it and then trim the wick (follow the instructions of the specific lamp you have). Now you are ready to light the lamp and recite the prayers and petitions a final time.

5. Burning: This form of setting lights is known as an "Eternal Flame" because you can continually fill the reservoir with the fuel for as long as it takes to claim victory in this matter.

6. Disposal: Once you are successful, clean out the base of the lamp and bury the ingredients respectfully either at a crossroads or close to your property. Then the lamp can be reused for a different working.

Double Action Reversing Candle

reversing black over red pillar candle	olotl
	olive oil
Agua Florida (page 26)	Sacred Resins Incense (page 175)
angelica (page 143)	
asafoetida	small mirror
rue (page 58)	small plate
basil (hot) (page 30)	petition
pericón (page 51)	parchment paper

Reversing black over red pillar candle: The black reverses all negativity and jinxes, and the red attracts our blessings.

Agua Florida: Used here to physically and spiritually clean the candle.

Angelica: See page 143.

Asafoetida (*Ferula assa-foetida*): Asafoetida is produced from the dried latex of the taproot from the *Ferula assa-foetida* bush, whose native range extends from eastern Iran to Afghanistan in central Asia. In culinary uses asafoetida, when cooked, mellows to an onion- or shallot-like flavor. (When smelled directly from the bag or jar, asafoetida emits an aroma of some pretty stank body odor, hence the English name of "devil's dung." A Bruja's trick to remove the smell from the fingers and hands is to wash them thoroughly with soap and water and then splash a little Agua Florida to break the fragrance and energies.) As a medicinal it acts as a relaxant, neuroprotective, memory enhancer, digestive tonic, antispasmodic, antioxidant, antimicrobial, and hepatoprotective (liver support) and has anticarcinogenic properties. In spiritual work asafoetida repels evil and malicious intents, breaks up long-standing bad luck and negativity intentionally directed at us, while being highly protective. "Spirit of Asafoetida, support us as we repel and break all negativity and negative thought patterns and energies, and expel all stagnation and bad luck from ourselves, our families, our spaces, and our lives. Be with us, Asafoetida, and elevate our awareness and consciousness to identify the sources of these energies, and aid us as we navigate around them. Be present and be strong within us and around us, Asafoetida."

Rue: See page 58.

Pericón: See page 51.

Olotl (*Zea mays*): Olotl is the heart of the ear of corn, the corncob, that has been dekerneled. Maize is a very sacred plant throughout the Americas and has medicinal and spiritual properties outside of its deliciousness. Every part of the corn plant has unique qualities, and corn silk has been employed for bladder infections, urinary tract inflammation, prostate inflammation, and kidney stones. The olotl or heart of the corn in Curanderismo and Brujería is a huge detoxifier (removes spiritual poisons that have been absorbed or ingested) and is also a spiritual helper for those suffering intense and painful menstrual cycles (limpias with olotl are common during these times). "Olotl, Heart of the Corn, please assist us as we detoxify and remove all poisons, toxins, cures, and negative witchcraft, whether known or unknown, from ourselves, our bodies, hearts, minds, and Spirits, and protect us and our families from harm. Sacred Medicine and Spirit of the Ancestors, support us as we find our balance, and bless us with vitality and life. Be with us, Olotl, and be in our work."

Olive oil (*Olea europaea*): Indigenous throughout the Mediterranean, olive trees have a long history of allyship throughout the world. Medicinally, olive and olive oil reduce blood sugar, cholesterol, and uric acid within the body as well as having antiviral properties (helps to identify and kill diseased and infected cells before they reproduce). As a spiritual advocate, olive is deeply connected to divinities and divine emanations. The olive is said to symbolize the intensity of our devotional practices and our ability to be subsumed by grace (enter a state of no-thingness), while the oil draws down the emanating light of the Creator and sits us in our deep heart wisdoms. (My first teachers utilized olive oil for their base in making their condition oils because of its sacred properties.) "Spirit of Olive Oil, be with us as we cleanse and clear all energies, situations, and people who do not serve our best interests or have our best intents at heart. Just as the olive is pressed to become oil, let all oppressions, pains, and suffering be squeezed and pressed out of ourselves and our spaces so we can move closer to the emanating light of the Creator and our Ancestors. Be with us, Olive Oil, in our hearts, minds, and Spirits, and be present in our work."

Sacred Resins Incense: See https://ulyssespress.com/books/the-modern-art-of-brujeria for a link to additional content.

Mirror: We use mirrors to reflect negative people and forces away from us, as well as in blessing work to reflect the positive energies into the world (visualize how a lighthouse amplifies and reflects its light).

1. Every time you start any work, first cleanse all of the ingredients and tools.

2. Write the petition, fold it three times away from yourself (which represents all the negativity being sent away from you), smoke it in the Sacred Resins Incense, and place it on the plate.

3. Consecrating the mirror: Using olive oil, anoint the four corners and the center of the mirror while verbally speaking your petition and prayers, then smoke it using the Sacred Resins Incense (while praying again), and finally, place it on top of the petition.

4. Creating the herbal blend: Utilizing the above recipe, make ¼ cup of the blend, pray over it with your petition, and blow on it gently three times to give it the breath of life. (Feel free to grind it into a powder if the mood strikes.) Then lay out a piece of parchment paper and sprinkle the whole mixture on it.

5. Rolling the candle: First, take the candle and pray over it to start to get the juices flowing. Next, carefully douse it in olive oil (some Brujas get very particular about this step: they hold it by the wick and move their hands down the candle to its base while visualizing all the negativity moving from their head and being squeezed out of their feet) and pray. Now lay the candle on the paper and roll it back and forth in order to pick up all the herbs and magical goodness that you have already created.

6. Placement: As the final step, first place the candle on the mirror. An easy trick to help it to stand is to heat the bottom of the candle with a lighter and then quickly and firmly place the candle in the middle of the mirror. (You don't know how many times I've almost set things on fire because the candle tipped over due to it not being firmly set on the mirror.) After the placement gather the remainder of your herbal mixture and sprinkle it in a counterclockwise circle (representing the energies reversing) while speaking aloud the petition and praying.

7. Lighting: As you light the candle, speak aloud the petition and pray. (It's repetitive for a reason: all of your intents and prayers are continually reiterated throughout the work. The candle is like the battery, and your prayers and petitions are what the battery is feeding.) At this point you can have the incense going as you pray (another form of reiterating the intents and prayers). As mentioned in the workings above, you don't have to keep it burning all the time, but remember to extinguish it versus blowing it out. (I've blown out spell candles before and haven't noticed a difference, but that's what I've been taught.

8. Disposal: This working is about reversing negativity, and in that vein, the remains of the burn are seen as the spiritual poo that you just squeezed out of the body. This instance is one of the only times that you should dispose of it in the trash (throw it in a trash can away from home because you don't want it around you) or bury it at a crossroads (where two roads meet that don't point home).

Tapa la Boca

Tapa la boca or "cover the mouth" closes the mouths of gossipers and busybodies who are overly involved in your personal affairs and helps stop the spread of rumors and lies.

lemon (page 38)

alum

camphor (page 59)

snake plant leaf

rue (page 58)

agrimony (page 100)

white chime candle

needle

thread

olive oil or Stop Gossip Oil

small plate

serrated kitchen knife

parchment paper

Lemon: See page 38.

Alum: Alum is a mineral compound consisting of a double sulfate, salt and aluminum. Alum was once used as an antiperspirant in deodorants, but in the 1980s it was discovered that it was carcinogenic over time when applied to the skin. In this recipe Alum is employed to cause the puckering of the gossiper's mouth in order to keep it shut. "Spirit of Alum, assist us as we close the mouths of all known and unknown gossipers. Remove our names from their tongues and shut them up. Be strong and present in this work, Spirit of Alum."

Camphor: See page 59.

Snake plant leaf (*Dracaena trifasciata*): Indigenous to tropical West Africa from Nigeria east to the Congo, snake plant is an "ornamental" (only for folks who aren't magical) house plant that is common across the Americas and Europe. In recent studies by NASA, the snake plant has been shown to filter out a large amount of air pollutants and to help reoxygenate spaces. In Malaysian traditional medicine the snake plant is mashed into a poultice to treat earaches, fevers, boils, and swelling. Spiritually, the snake plant is connected to the energies of blades and swords, cutting through energetic knots and severing negative bonds, while also being highly protective and a guardian of the home. "Spirit of Snake Plant, Sword of Truth, Justice, and Protection, help us to cut the tongues of malicious gossipers and show them the results of their actions. Snake Plant, guard us against untrue and hurtful language and remove our names from the mouths of those who would meddle in our affairs. Spirit of the Snake Plant, be strong, present, and attentive in this working."

Rue: See page 58.

Agrimony: See page 100.

White chime candle: These candles are 4" tall and ½" wide with an average burn time of 2–2½ hours each.

Needle and thread: You will cut the lemon in half, load it, and then sew it up with the thread, symbolizing that the gossiper's mouth has been sewn shut.

Olive oil or Stop Gossip Oil: You can find store-made Stop Gossip Oil at most botanicas or metaphysical shops, and olive oil can be used as well.

1. Clean and cleanse all ingredients.

2. Petition writing: Taking a small strip of the snake plant, write your petition on it, anoint it with the condition oil in each of the four corners and the middle of the strip, and place it to the side.

3. Cutting and loading the lemon: Next, anoint the knife with the condition oil while verbally reciting the petition, and then cut the lemon in half. (This represents cutting the tongues of the gossipers and those who speak negatively against you.) Now load each of the ingredients and the condition oil into both halves of the lemon while praying. Finally, twist the strip of snake plant that was placed to the side and skewer the halves together.

4. Sewing it shut: Thread the needle and anoint the whole string with oil while praying that those who are gossiping will close their mouths and keep them shut. Now sew the whole lemon back together while praying.

5. Loading and rolling the candle: Similar to the Double Action Reversing Candle, anoint the candle with the oil while moving your hands downward toward the base (remembering to imagine all the gossip and negativity being pushed out of the body) and pray. Next, roll the candle in the remaining herbs and minerals.

6. Burning the candle: After the candle has been dressed and prayed over, light it and use the drippings to completely seal the whole lemon in wax. (At a certain point it will become hard to hold and you can securely place it on top of the seams that have just been sewn up to finish the remainder of the burn.)

7. Disposal: After the wax has dried, take it to a moving body of water (a river, ocean, stream, or any water that moves), pray over it (to have the gossipers move away from you), and throw it as far away as possible into the water. Thank the Spirits of River for assisting in the work and leave an offering (pocket change, something sweet, or a bit of tobacco). Walk away and don't look back.

8. Refreshing yourself after: While this is not cursing work, it definitely has a bit of an energetic edge, and I highly recommend taking a mild uncrossing bath like the Grocery Store Cleansing Bath (page 96).

Activist and Protestor Protection

1 red seven-day glass-encased candle

4 gold or yellow pillar candles

Agua Florida (page 26)

angelica (page 143)

goldenseal (page 148)

echinacea (page 138)

High John root (page 138)

black cat hair

lemongrass (page 59)

tobacco (page 63)

camphor (page 59)

sandalwood (page 54)

yerba buena/mint (page 32)

rue (page 58)

1 pinch of salt

olive oil (page 175)   petition

butter knife   serving plate

parchment paper

Red seven-day glass-encased candle: Representative of the activist and the resources they need to be strengthened, safe, and invisible before all seen and unseen aggressors, counterprotestors, and police.

Gold or yellow pillar candles: These will be our guardians, protectors, sentinels, and guides for the activist to surround them in their energies and protect them from harm.

Angelica: See page 143.

Goldenseal: See page 148.

Echinacea: See page 138.

High John root: See page 138.

Black cat hair: In magical traditions in the Americas, black cats have the energies of stealth, luck, invisibility, and stalking prey and are inherently connected with the unseen and supernatural worlds. "Spirit of Black Cats, assist us, guide us, and protect us as we fight for justice, equality, human worth and value, and global care and upliftment. Aid us, Black Cats, to be invisible before all enemies, counterprotestors, and law enforcement officials who seek to disrupt and cause harm. Help us to quietly gather our forces, be stealthy with our plans, and silently position ourselves to pounce when the timing is right. Spirit of Black Cats, support this work, support our cause, and be an ally in our fights. Be with us, Black Cat, as we claim victory and success."

Lemongrass: See page 59.

Tobacco: See page 63.

Camphor: See page 59.

Sandalwood: See page 54.

Yerba buena/mint: See page 32.

Rue: See page 58.

Olive oil: See page 175.

Salt: See page 97.

1. Clean and cleanse everything.

2. Sealing: Anoint the plate in each of the four corners while verbally praying and speaking the petition.

3. Petition writing: Following the instructions on page 179, write the petition and then place in the middle of the plate.

4. Creating the load for the red candle: Mix angelica, goldenseal, echinacea, High John root, lemongrass, tobacco, and the black cat hair, add a splash or two of the olive oil, pray over it and speak your petition aloud, and then set this aside.

5. Creating the load for the guardian candles: Mix angelica, tobacco, camphor, sandalwood, mint, rue, and the pinch of salt together, add a splash or two of olive oil, and verbally pray.

6. Loading the red candle: This candle represents the activists and is the center of the work. Using the butter knife, carefully carve out a pocket where you can place the load (see page 161 for details on this process). Next, add the mixture, then another small splash of olive oil, pray and speak aloud your petition, and then cover the magical load with the remainder of the carved-out wax. Next, pray and speak aloud the petition one final time, breathe three times into the candle, knock it three times, trim the wick, and place the candle on the petition paper in the middle of the plate.

7. Rolling the gold/yellow pillar candles: Taking the parchment paper, sprinkle the herbal mixture on top and add a small splash of olive oil. Next, anoint the candles, but this time you will be using your hands to draw up from the base all the way to the wick (you are drawing protection to you, so imagine these energies rising from your feet all the way to your head). Now roll the candles in the mixture, verbally speaking your prayer and petitions, breathe on them three times, heat them a bit at their base with a lighter to secure them to the plate in the four directions surrounding the red, glass-encased candle, and finally, trim the wicks.

8. Light it up: Now you are ready to begin the ritual. Light the middle candle and verbally say the name or names of the people you would like to enshroud in protection, then say your prayers and petitions over the candle and visualize the types of experiences and feelings you would like them to have as activists and protestors doing the work. Next, light the four guardian candles and ask that they assist, guard, guide, and act as sentinels while the activists and protestors are in the field. Then visualize and imagine the ways that your people will be guarded and guided. (Some Brujas like to burn dragon's blood or a protective incense to further fortify the work.)

9. Disposal: I love to take the candle remains and put them in a little charm bag for the person to carry as they do their work. You can also bury the remains in the backyard of the organizational headquarters or in a potted plant in the office.

RESOURCES

Books

Albuquerque, Ulysses Paulino, Umesh Patil, and Ákos Máthé, eds. *Medicinal and Aromatic Plants of South America*. New York: Springer, 2018.

Chatroux, Sylvia Seroussi. *Botanica Poetica*. Ashland: Poetica Press, 2004.

Crane, Justine. *Working the Bench: A Natural Botanical Perfumery Instructional for Beginners*. Scotts Valley, CA: CreateSpace, 2013.

Duke, James A. *Duke's Handbook of Medicinal Plants of Latin America*. Boca Raton, FL: CRC Press, 2009.

Garrett, J. T. *The Cherokee Herbal: Native Plant Medicine from the Four Directions*. Rochester, VT: Inner Traditions, Bear & Company, 2003.

Light, Phyllis D. 2018. *Southern Folk Medicine: Healing Traditions from the Appalachian Fields and Forests*. Berkeley, CA: North Atlantic Books.

McCabe, James. *The Language and Sentiment of Flowers*. Carlisle, MA: Applewood Books, 2003.

Moriel, Ayala. *Foundations of Natural Perfumery*. Vancouver, BC: Ayala Moriel Parfums, 2015.

Quiros-Moran, Dalia. *Guide to Afro-Cuban Herbalism*. Bloomington, IN: AuthorHouse, 2003.

Torres, Eliseo. *Curandero: A Life in Mexican Folk Healing*. Albuquerque: University of New Mexico Press, 2005.

Torres, Eliseo. *Healing with Herbs and Rituals*. Albuquerque: University of New Mexico Press, 2006.

Herbal Resources

Apothecary Tinctura, www.apothecarytinctura.com

Rosehouse Botanicals, www.rosehousebotanicals.com

Scarlet Sage, scarletsage.com

Starwest Botanicals, www.starwest-botanicals.com

Strictly Medicinal Seeds, strictlymedicinalseeds.com

Essential Oils and Perfumery

Providence Perfume, www.providenceperfume.com

Eden's Botanical, www.edenbotanicals.com

Perfumer's Apprentice, shop.perfumersapprentice.com

Lou's Offerings

If you are interested in my community offerings and teachings, please feel free to check out some of the resources below.

Water Has No Enemy, www.facebook.com/WaterHasNoEnemy.org

Spiritual readings and divinations, Brujería classes: www.louflorez.com

WitchCraft, monthly celebrations of writing and rituals honoring the full moon, Instagram @Witch-Craft.999999999

For a taste of some of my magical offerings, try Violet Moon Tea produced by Rosehouse Botanicals or my Violet Moon Perfume sold through my website.

Lou's Brujería Spotify Playlist, https://open.spotify.com/playlist/1AO8hDZzZcOTHMU4cQY8XN?si=90a794f6954b4f21

ACKNOWLEDGMENTS

This book would not be possible without the continued support and love of my family, Elders, and beloved community. To my mother and father, Romana and Louis, and to all the Ancestors who are celebrating this accomplishment, it is their guidance, support, and love that has taught me how to embody these medicines in myself and for my community. I give thanks to Nick, RJ, Leticia, and Harishabd who are my heart and who's wisdom, advice, and companionship in this journey has driven me to elevate my work and my life. I would also like to honor all the Señoras and magical beings who have kept these traditions alive and who continue to work on behalf of the betterment of the world.

Gratitude and deep appreciation to Eliot Reynolds for pushing me forward in this project and for being a book doula and constant positive force as I completed this work. Thank you to my Elders and Teachers—Iyanifa Ifalade Love Ta'shia Asanti, Mariah Prosper, Sharon Varner, Loraine Fox Davis, Iya Tabia, and Selah Saterstrom—and to all the traditional and magical herbalists (especially Lynn Flanagan-Till, Maurice Ka, Nicole Smith Johnson, and Ruta Lauleva), medicine makers, aunties, and diviners who have shared their wisdom, knowledge, and hearts.

ABOUT THE AUTHOR

Lou Florez (Awo Ifadunsin) is an internationally known Bruje/witch, medicine maker, herbalist, spirit worker, priest, activist, and artist who has studied with indigenous communities and elders throughout the globe. His teachings and practice are grounded in prompting connectedness to the body through physical, emotional, spiritual, and environmental landscapes, creating living, dynamic relationships so we can become conscious of the inherent power available to us in every lived second.

Lou's writings have been featured on Remezcla (2020), *The Wild Hunt* (2017), and *Bringing Race to the Table: Exploring Racism in the Pagan Community* (2015). He also cofounded WitchCraft (2020), a monthly online gathering dedicated to the full moon and composed of poetry and witchcraft experiments.

Lou's work promotes spiritual activation and social empowerment. He is the executive director and cofounder of Water Has No Enemy, a nonprofit organization committed to healing justice, where he creates transformational dialogues focused on reclaiming indigenous wisdom through healing our relationships to self, others, and the natural world.

As a presiding priest of Ile Ori Ogbe Egun (2021), an international IFA temple honoring Orisha from a global perspective, Lou creates Orisha-centered fellowship, services, and programming rooted in liberative theology and practices. Lou facilitates workshops and hands-on teaching opportunities on Brujería, herbalism, and hoodoo and lectures on the intersectional meeting grounds of art, activism, and witchcraft at universities and colleges. He also produces and curates a line of artisanal, Brujería-based perfumes, oils, and baths, and runs a cooperative, Los Angeles-based medicine garden.

For more information on Lou and his work, visit www.louflorez.com.